# ABRAHAM

## HOW TAMING OUR BIBLE HEROES BLINDS US TO THE WILD WAYS OF GOD

## CHRIS TIEGREEN

SALT**RIVER**

AN IMPRINT OF TYNDALE HOUSE PUBLISHERS, INC.

Visit Tyndale's exciting Web site at www.tyndale.com

*TYNDALE* is a registered trademark of Tyndale House Publishers, Inc.

*SaltRiver* and the SaltRiver logo are registered trademarks of Tyndale House Publishers, Inc.

*Fixing Abraham: How Taming Our Bible Heroes Blinds Us to the Wild Ways of God*

Designed by Rule29

Published in association with the literary agency of Mark Sweeney & Associates.

**Library of Congress Cataloging-in-Publication Data**

Tiegreen, Chris.
    Fixing Abraham : how taming our Bible heroes blinds us to the wild ways of God / Chris Tiegreen.
       p. cm.
    Includes bibliographical references and index.
    ISBN 978-1-4143-2172-1 (sc : alk. paper)
    1. Bible—Biography. 2. Christian life—Biblical teaching. I. Title.
    BS571.T54 2009
    220.9′2—dc22                                 2008042114

Printed in the United States of America

15   14   13   12   11   10   09
7    6    5    4    3    2    1

# CONTENTS

# INTRODUCTION

I knew it would happen eventually. I just didn't think it would be so soon. After all, I had made a serious vow long ago: never would I get sucked into an online debate by posting a comment after someone's article. But I slipped up, and the ensuing melee consumed half my week.

Yes, I know. I shouldn't have broken my vow. But the temptation was irresistible as the statements of the author were practically screaming for clarification. And then the "post your comments" link at the bottom of the article just glared at me—a steely, piercing, relentless stare—for what seemed like eternity. I refused, vehemently at times, but it wouldn't be moved. Eventually, I blinked.

The article in question was one evangelical writer's critique on what he considered gushy worship music that portrayed God as having romantic love for his people. He took the lyrics of a popular song and picked them apart, blasting away at the unfounded ideas contained in each line. He emphasized the majesty and holiness of God and our rather severe need for justification by faith. God's love, he said, is not gooey. We aren't loveable, and the almighty Creator doesn't yearn for us. He saves us because we need saving, but we've watered down the gospel by exchanging his loving-kindness for romantic mush. And that, in his opinion, has no biblical basis whatsoever.

I understand, of course, what the writer's concerns were. He was reacting against what can sometimes seem like overfamiliarity with the sovereign Lord and righteous Judge of the universe. He lamented the fact that many people have a much-too-casual approach to God and never realize the holy ground they stand on. And I agree that this is an important point to make. What bothered me was his sarcastic and condescending tone toward some songwriters who are genuine Christians and really do seem to love God—*and* who were using an entirely biblical image. I couldn't let his insulting verbiage or some of his unfounded and unbiblical overstatements go unchallenged.

So I challenged them. I quoted verse after verse illustrating that God presents himself in Scripture as the Husband of his people and Jesus as the Bridegroom of the church. I cited many passages from the Psalms and prophets that reveal God's tender heart toward us, and I pointed out the pervasive interpretation throughout history by both Jewish and Christian theologians of the Song of Songs as an allegory of God's love for his people. With great satisfaction, I thought, *Yes, the Bible is clearly on my side. The critics will have nothing to say in response.*

Surprisingly, most didn't get the point. In fact, I was amazed at some of the responses to all of the biblical examples and quotes I and other like-minded posters provided. "That's unbiblical!" one said. "This is a blasphemous idea," wrote another. "We're really on dangerous ground when we try to remake God in our image like this," warned several.

So I posted another response, in which I cited the Jewish interpretation of the Sinai covenant as a betrothal ceremony, an interpretation found even within the pages of the Bible itself (see Jeremiah 2:2; 3:8-14; 31:32; and Ezekiel 16:8, for example).[1] I reminded other participants in the discussion that Israel's idolatry was quite often referred to as "adultery," that God said he would rejoice over his people as a bridegroom rejoices over his bride, that God does use the language of yearning and brokenheartedness in numerous places in Scripture, that prophets like Ezekiel and Hosea used rather graphic terms and lifestyles to illustrate the romantic heart of God, and that the Bible and history culminate with a wedding. I made it clear: this is not a minor biblical theme.

And because the author of the article and many others who posted responses seemed to feel that this idea of a romantic God is a newfangled plague sweeping across a compromising, pseudo-Christian church, I cited great figures of Christian history like Jonathan Edwards, Charles Spurgeon, and Hudson Taylor, who all saw this romantic imagery and interpreted the Song of Songs as a picture of God's love.

What I found most fascinating was my critics' contention that I was picking and choosing Bible verses according to my faulty understanding and ignorance of the plain teaching of Scripture. In other words, all of my Bible quotes, though by no means taken out of context, were unbiblical.

That's like a friend I once knew who thought Jesus' declarations of woe on the religious leaders weren't very Christlike. I'm pretty sure that the definition of Christlike is being like Christ, and since Jesus is the Christ, then by definition he's Christlike. Same goes for all the Scripture references I pointed out. The fact that they were taken directly from the Bible kind of qualifies them as biblical.

But my detractors didn't see it that way. They have every right to agree with the underlying purpose of the original article and to disagree with the tone of the song in question, but they have no case when they start calling Bible verses unbiblical. When people are so set in their theology that they think Scripture is unscriptural—*and* call an obvious biblical theme *nonsense* and *garbage*—something is seriously wrong.

I joke about my online experience, but it's really a symptom of an alarming problem. Somehow we've developed a system of norms that is derived from the Bible but fails to capture the spirit of the Bible. We know detailed chapters and verses without grasping major themes. (Case in point: One of the commentators in that discussion informed me that he had done a word search and

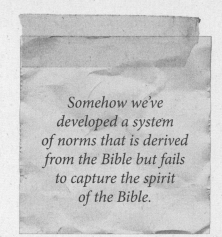

*Somehow we've developed a system of norms that is derived from the Bible but fails to capture the spirit of the Bible.*

the word *romantic* did not appear in any version of the Bible. Therefore, it wasn't biblical. Meanwhile, huge portions of the prophets and wisdom literature remained unaddressed.) This is why some of our doctrinal discussions turn into either/or debates. In my experience, Christians typically gravitate toward one of two extremes: God is holy, awesome, majestic, and righteous; or he's gentle, tender, intimate, comforting, and loving. Isn't it obvious from Scripture that he's all of that and more? Both ends of that spectrum are well attested in the Bible. Yet our mental framework often tries to force one or the other, because apparently he can't fit both descriptions in the same human mind. Does God save us for his glory or because he loves us deeply? Are his thoughts infinitely higher than ours, or do we have the mind of Christ? Does he save us from our sin or our loneliness? Is he strong and mighty or tender and affectionate? People actually choose sides about such things—and claim, rather stridently, that theirs is the biblical view.

But apart from the possibility of initiating or getting pulled into some heated online debates, what's the danger of adhering strictly to our understanding of biblical principles? Aren't biblical principles essential? Don't they keep us on the straight and narrow? Don't we need some clear definitions about what we do and don't believe?

In one sense, this is true. Holding fast to these standards can prevent us from getting sucked into the false doctrines of a cult. They help us focus on the essentials of our faith. They keep us anchored in truth.

But these benefits can also become a real problem. In preventing us from hearing the strange doctrines of a cult, they also immunize us from any radical, paradigm-shifting messages from God. In keeping us focused on essentials, they make us vigilant and even obsessive about what an "essential" is—which can turn out to be any minor doctrinal detail—and cause us to split with believers who happen to have a different set of "essentials." And in keeping us anchored in truth, they can keep us anchored—period. Even when the Spirit wants to move us.

Though our principles may give us a sense of safety and prevent us from making some wrong moves, they can also give us the false impression that we've got it all figured out. The result is an air of smugness filled with the unpleasant odor of misdirected zeal, and it's hardly attractive or helpful to those who are hurting—or even to those who simply crave a dynamic relationship with a nonformulaic God. People who are struggling generally have questions that aren't easily answered by broad scriptural principles. We need a personal touch. And hyperdoctrinalism is anything but personal.

Let me be emphatic up front that I'm not arguing against doctrine. The Bible spells out some absolutes for us that can't be compromised.[2] Nevertheless, the voice of God almost always stretches us beyond what we thought we understood. The more specifically we try to set in stone what we understand, the more shattered we'll be when God tries to interact with us. When we assume we can anticipate how life will work out, we'll eventually be disillusioned with our faith. Circumstances, the sovereignty of God, and the dynamics of the Holy Spirit can get pretty messy.

*Circumstances, the sovereignty of God, and the dynamics of the Holy Spriit can get pretty messy.*

If you do with doctrinal definitions what the Pharisees did with the law of Moses, you'll probably miss out on some adventures with God. You won't have "ears that hear" when he calls you out of your comfort zone and invites you to participate in some unique avenue of Kingdom building. You'll also be less likely to encourage others who are being challenged by the Holy Spirit to step out in faith. In fact, in many cases, you'll actually discourage them. Why? Because "God wouldn't/doesn't/can't" do what they think his voice is telling them.

I have a friend, for example, who has sensed God calling her to leave a ministry organization to put herself through cosmetology school so she could minister to women about their potential beauty and identity in Christ as she's beautifying their outward appearance. To me, that sounds like a wonderfully creative mission that comes straight out of God's heart, but she has had to listen to "deep concerns" over her plans. If she heeded all this godly, biblical advice—"You're too gifted for this," "I'm worried about your faith"—she would try to deny herself and crucify that desire. But if the desire came from God in the first place, wouldn't that be tragic?

Our tendency to stick doggedly to our expectations of how God is supposed to work is remarkably reminiscent of a certain group of priests, scribes, and religious scholars who lived about two thousand years ago. They used a very similar approach to determine that the teachings and works of a particular Messiah could not have been from God. Their reasoning? What he said and did wasn't scriptural. There were no specific references authorizing some of the claims he made. In fact, several aspects of his ministry seemed to directly contradict the plain teaching of Scripture. Therefore, he was a false teacher. And because his claims were so extravagant, his false teachings were blasphemous. So he was summarily executed.

## FENCING THE GOSPEL

Don't misunderstand: I believe in the absolutes of Scripture, and I'm deeply committed to the fact that God breathed his Word into the people who wrote it. It's all true, from Genesis to Revelation. But let me also emphasize that I wholeheartedly stand behind the absolutes *of Scripture*, not the assumptions of evangelical culture, of historic Christianity's time-honored interpretations, or of our various expressions of systematic theology or denominational practice—what I refer to from now on as "biblical principles."

These can involve doctrinal definitions, but I'm thinking more specifically of the set of principles that cause us to write books, preach sermons, lead Bible studies, and so on, that focus on "how to _____." Topics like "Six steps to effective prayer," with the implication that God rarely or never hears prayers that miss one of the steps; "How to heal broken relationships," as though anyone who follows these biblical principles will get along with everyone; or "When God speaks, he will always _____," as if God's voice could be reduced to a formula to figure out. We make a lot of assumptions when we turn guidelines into formulas, and those assumptions easily become sacred. We then find ourselves having a wonderful relationship with principles rather than a wonderful relationship with God. And only the latter will satisfy, because we were never designed for the former.

> *We make a lot of assumptions when we turn guidelines into formulas, and those assumptions easily become sacred.*

It's not that I think these principles are always wrong. All of them can be accurate and helpful—to a point—and all have significantly shaped my Christian growth in positive ways. But we have to understand them for what they are—guidelines derived from Scripture—rather than as the scriptural answer for such-and-such a problem. I don't believe in our infallibility as interpreters of God's Word, and I'm convinced that we often approach it in much the same manner as some scribes and priests did a couple thousand years ago. We end up with a well-developed Christianity that has little room for Christ.

Here's an example of what I mean. God gave Israel the Torah (the law and teachings of the first five books of the Bible), which included some very specific commandments for righteous behavior and forms of worship. Because God's warnings against breaking his commandments were rather strong, over the course of time ancient rabbis instituted quite a few laws as a "fence" around the Torah. These were their binding instructions that would protect people from getting too close to breaking God's commandments. For example, the laws for Sabbath forbid work on the seventh day of each week, but a rabbinic law forbids picking up an implement of work. Why? Because the one holding it might accidentally use it before remembering that it was the Sabbath, thereby breaking the original commandment. So over time, layers and layers of such boundaries were placed around God's law and actually became laws themselves. Whenever someone—let's say Jesus, for example—broke one, he would be charged with doing something unbiblical, even though only the original law was in the Bible.

I think many Christians do the same thing today, both literally and figuratively. One example of the literal sense involves the principle of not causing a fellow believer to sin (derived from 1 Corinthians 8:1-13). I've encountered various cautions along these lines, ranging from the obvious (like not offering an alcoholic a drink) to the hardly necessary (like forbidding men from wearing shorts when they play church-league softball because there might be a woman nearby who has a thing for calf muscles). Most, of course, fall somewhere in between these extremes.

Developing an extrabiblical behavioral norm is one thing, but the figurative ways we fence the Word raise the stakes considerably if they constrain the Spirit. For example, we know that many can be enticed from godly living by their own desires[3] and that the world and its desires are passing away,[4] so we've developed a theology that comes very close to saying that our desires are so misleading that they must always be sacrificed for God's will—which, of course, assumes that his will is usually the polar opposite of our desire. It's true that our desires can be misleading, but that's not the only side of the story; if we delight in the Lord he gives us the desires of our heart,[5] and if we live in fellowship with him, we can ask whatever we wish and it will be done for us.[6] We're so afraid of people abusing that privilege—that's always a possibility—that we throw lots of cold water on the fire of those promises. The problem is that it isn't always *biblical* cold water, but it still effectively puts out the fire in those who would otherwise believe that perhaps a deep desire was given to them by God. Countless Christians are currently trying to crucify a desire that God put in their hearts in the first place. Why? Because we've drawn boundaries around the dangerous truth and said, "Believe it, but don't get too close."

This "death to all personal desire" is just one example of the many evangelical ideals we've developed. Many of these ideals have reached mythical status as an overarching, self-evident truth of Scripture, though a closer look at other related passages shows them to be anything but self-evident. We're right to want to adhere to the principles set forth in God's Word, yet we need to admit that God does not always act as we expect him to. We can see evidence of that if we reread passages about the prophets, the apostles, and Jesus himself and then honestly evaluate our reaction to their words and deeds. Based on our assumptions about how God works, we would have more than enough wise advice to fix people like Abraham, David, Isaiah, and Paul. If they walked into our churches today, we would counsel them not only against the flaws they had and the mistakes they made, but also against the things God told them to do. We wouldn't tolerate their obedience because it wouldn't look like obedience to us.

In the characters of the Bible, we have enough evidence to undo the following Christian myths:

+ Desiring anything other than God himself is unspiritual.
+ Worshiping God for the benefits we get from him is unspiritual.
+ The Holy Spirit's work will never confuse us or contradict our biblical principles.
+ God won't answer our prayers if they're mixed with impure motives.
+ God doesn't speak to us in dreams or visions anymore.
+ Embarrassing behavior doesn't come from God. It comes from the world, the flesh, or the devil.
+ God doesn't want you to base your faith on someone else's experience. If he wants you to believe a truth contained in someone's testimony, he'll prove it to you directly.
+ Any guidance that hints of immorality is not from God.
+ When you find yourself standing alone against the advice of godly counsel, you can be sure you're not following God.
+ God wants us to have faith, but he doesn't want us to be unreasonable.

I realize that many of these are valuable beliefs that have helped a lot of people, but they aren't infallible rules that can be universally applied to everyone across the board. They are good principles derived from biblical truth, but they aren't biblical truth itself. And in some cases, they're just wrong. I'll demonstrate why in the pages of this book, as we see how dangerous our wisdom can be when used as a blanket for everyone. But that's the unfortunate nature of principles; they don't bend with each situation.[7] They cause us to make incorrect judgments of people who deviate from them.

## IT'S A MATTER OF PRINCIPLE

A more significant problem is this: these principles can quickly and silently become the substance of our faith. As Frederick Buechner has said, in unapologetic bluntness, "Principles are what people have instead of God."[8] That's tragic, because the substance of our faith should be a real, dynamic relationship with the Holy Spirit who lives in us.

God gives us a great illustration of how we are to be guided by the movement of the Spirit in the way he led Israel in the wilderness. He never allowed them to develop a set of guidelines for wilderness wandering. "In all the travels of the Israelites, whenever the cloud lifted from above the tabernacle, they would set out; but if the cloud did not lift, they did not set out—until the day it lifted" (Exodus 40:36-37, NIV). Neither would he allow them to stock up on manna—except, of course, on the day before the Sabbath, in which case stocking up for the extra day was perfectly fine. He had given them plenty of rules and regulations, and they were to obey them strictly. That consistency is an important part of following him. But the law was not the substance of their relationship with him. Obedience to a written code of conduct could never become a substitute for obedience to his voice. He had called them and delivered them before establishing his commandments, and he insisted that they follow whenever and wherever he led. In very irregular movements, he gave them personal guidance that wasn't contained in the law.

Jesus essentially said the same of people who follow him. "The wind blows wherever it pleases. You hear its sound, but you cannot tell where it comes from or where it is going. So it is with everyone born of the Spirit" (John 3:8, NIV).[9] That verse is more than a little problematic for most Christians, because we like to know where things are coming from and where they are going. We don't like the uncertainty of a spiritual life without well-defined parameters. But Jesus made it abundantly clear—in these words, in his ministry, and through the movements of his Spirit in Acts—that the Christian life is not predictable. We can never say "This is how God always works" or "God wouldn't say something like that" unless we know for certain all the details of a situation *and* are talking about his absolute, unchanging, clearly revealed attributes. Like it or not, there's no formula for following the Spirit. Guidelines, yes. But no formulas.

Jesus made this point when some rigid disciples of the law pointed out that he and his followers were violating the clear dictates of Scripture by gathering some grain to eat on the Sabbath. And they were right; he *was* breaking a clear scriptural principle. Jesus could have told them that their understanding of the law was completely off base, but he didn't. Neither did he give his followers license to disregard the law at will; instead, he simply informed the Jewish leaders that breaking that law had a clear scriptural precedent. When David and his companions were hungry, they went into God's house and ate sacred, dedicated bread—bread that had been offered to God according to the requirement of the law. No one was allowed to touch that bread but a priest, and then only under certain conditions. Jesus was clear: this "was not lawful for them to do" (Matthew 12:4, NIV). But David and his companions did eat it, God approved, and Jesus held him up as a positive example. That's unpredictable and way beyond formulas.

That doesn't fit the religious convictions of most committed Christians today. That's because discipleship in much of contemporary Christianity is largely a seminar-type process. We go to lectures—we usually call them sermons—where we sit passively and learn. Then, if we're diligent and committed, we fill in the gaps between sessions with our own study of the Bible and related materials. We like clear definitions, so even when God doesn't offer them, we come up with some and enforce them.

Our faith becomes a matter of knowing the right things and, one would hope, putting them into practice. God's Word goes into the mind and out through the mouth, the hands, and the feet. Rarely are emotions or intuitive perceptions considered an integral part of the disciple's walk because those things aren't measurable and accurate. (Neither is our objective reasoning, by the way.) So while we may be encouraged to spend time listening for God's voice, we're warned against putting too much faith in the words we sense the Spirit is speaking to us.

# WHAT *IS* JESUS DOING?

There's no legitimate Christian alternative to an ongoing, dynamic, conversational relationship with God. That's why "What would Jesus do?" is usually the wrong question to be asking. It sounds awfully hypothetical for someone who's interacting with us in some pretty intimate ways. The better question is, "What *is* Jesus doing?" An even better question is, "Jesus, what are you doing right now in this situation, and what role do you want me to have in it?" Actually, that's two questions in one. But this does a much better job of acknowledging that your relationship with God is actually a relationship.

We evangelicals are great at emphasizing this need to have a personal relationship with God, but we blow a gasket when someone's relationship gets personal in unconventional ways. In reality, too often we advocate a close but supervised connection with God, not a deeply personal experience. For example, quite a few Christians get really nervous when someone says God spoke to them, even though two-way communication is integral to any real relationship. In some circles, any offering to God that is much less or much more than 10 percent of gross income is highly suspicious for its weak faith, on the one hand, or its excessive zeal, on the other—even though any real relationship rises and falls in intensity and varies in its needs and demands, depending on the season. In our desire for a consistent walk with God, we far too often strive for a predictable walk and feel guilty when it doesn't happen. So for all our talk about personal relationships, apparently what we really want is for people to follow conventions and get to know a static God. And that is not biblical discipleship.

*Too often we advocate a close but supervised connection with God, not a deeply personal experience.*

Anything that puts your discipleship on cruise control inhibits a real relationship with God, and that includes a set of principles. It also includes a systematic theology that bends the Bible to fit its logic rather than bending its logic to fit the Bible.[10] Theology is certainly important, but we often turn it into a structure that the Bible doesn't support. We treat Scripture like a box full of puzzle pieces that we have to figure out how to put together. Haven't you ever wondered, though, why God didn't give us a systematic theology to begin with? He gave us an inspired collection of experiences and stories that express who he is without reducing him to definitions. I believe he gave us historical narratives and poetic wisdom and real-life experiences because our categorical thinking inevitably reduces him in our minds. If he spelled out our theology for us, we'd develop a relationship with the theology rather than with him. That's formulaic spirituality, and it deludes us into thinking we're relating to God when we're not. Whether it's theology, law, marriage, employment, friendship, or anything else, a rigid structure can squeeze the breath out of all that's good. "The letter kills, but the Spirit gives life."[11]

Our systematic tendencies often lead to a militant attitude when we encounter "unbiblical" ideas and unclear theology. Many evangelicals see themselves as troubleshooters, watchdogs on the prowl for any hint of doctrinal impurity.[12] We can be really condescending toward other Christians who don't see things the way we do. And a lot of times our logic about whether something is biblical or not comes out of thought processes that aren't biblical in themselves.

Here's one way that works: You've certainly heard the kind of logic that says something like, "If verse A says this, and verse B says that, then doctrine C is obvious." That's good, Greek, linear logic, and it can be helpful, but it isn't infallible logic in the Kingdom of God. For example, imagine you're a sincere teacher of God's law in Jesus' day.[13] The Law was very explicit in its prohibitions against eating the blood in animal meat, to the degree that the very idea of eating or drinking any amount of blood was considered grossly immoral. And this wasn't just a cultural taboo; it was divine law given at Mount Sinai by a thundering voice from heaven. "As for the life of all flesh, its blood is identified with its life. Therefore I said to the sons of Israel, 'You are not to eat the blood of any flesh, for the life of all flesh is its blood; whoever eats it shall be cut off'" (Leviticus 17:14).[14] With this firmly in your mind as an eternal, divine ordinance, imagine listening to Jesus teach one day and hearing the words, "Truly, truly, I say to you, unless you eat the flesh of the Son of Man *and drink His blood*, you have no life in yourselves.... For My flesh is true food, and *My blood is true drink*" (John 6:53, 55, italics added).

As a faithful, obedient follower of God, what would your response be? If you approach the situation with the thought processes and criteria almost universally applied in Christian circles today, you would be compelled to reject him. Defenders of the faith would say something along the lines of, "I'm not sure exactly what he means by that, but this is clear enough that we can safely say he's contradicting the revealed will of God. God says emphatically that consuming blood is strictly forbidden. This man says we must drink his blood. Even if he means it symbolically, it's a slap in the face of scriptural principles. Therefore, Jesus cannot possibly be the Messiah, because he's advocating something God has forbidden." And as a faithful believer in God's Word, that would make perfect sense to you. Someone's words might be an enigma, but you can always count on the plain meaning of Scripture to keep you anchored.

Can you see why most of the teachers of the law rejected the Savior himself, not just on the basis of this incident regarding the blood, but also because of his clear violations (in their minds) of the Sabbath, his abrasive words and frequent public confrontations, his propensity to participate in dinners where a lot of alcohol was being served, his extremely arrogant claims, and so on? This kind of thinking might lead any of us today to miss the Messiah too.

## SEEING WITH GOD'S EYES

Why is this so important? Because, I believe, we are in an age when the strange and marvelous works of God are on the rise. God is pouring out on his people fresh insights about himself and his ways—not new truth, but new perspectives and deeper understanding of the truth. Like a brilliant, multifaceted diamond, the truth that has always been there displays its beauty in new ways when under a different light, or against a different background, or with newly developed technology to study it. The diamond hasn't changed, but its visual manifestations sometimes do. As the age-old gospel is applied to modern situations, spiritual insight shifts and even expands. And externally, the Spirit seems to be showing his repertoire more prominently than during many other stages of church history. Reports of signs and miracles seem to be dramatically increasing in frequency. Along with this flowering of the Spirit's work are plenty of fake revelations and miracles; counterfeits always cling closely to the real thing. And that's where an authentic experience with the Spirit of God—that real relationship that can't be substituted with principles, as we'll explore throughout this book—becomes absolutely critical.

Many have rejected entire movements because they've noticed a few counterfeits. (Interestingly, they don't stop handling all U.S. currency when they've spotted a counterfeit bill, but this knee-jerk reaction seems perfectly normal when applied to spiritual issues.) The typical Christian response to unfamiliar movements of God is to come up with several verses that "clearly" dictate against it, interpret the statements of key people in the worst possible light, demonstrate how these people violate "the plain teaching of Scripture," and then marginalize any preacher/teacher who looks like, smells like, or talks like he or she has brushed up against that movement. And if you look closely enough in the Gospels, you'll see exactly the same approach applied to Jesus and his followers.

It is not possible in these days or in the future to apply biblical formulas to what God is doing. If we do, we'll miss him just as surely as the priesthood of Jesus' day missed the time of their visitation. No, an intellectual understanding of the Bible will only get us so far; if we really want to encounter him, we'll need to be open to the possibility that he may actually defy our expectations once in a while.

> He may use people who look foolish to see if he's more important
> to us than our own sense of sophistication.
> He may stretch our doctrinal understanding to see if we're more
> in love with the Spirit than we are with our education.
> He may pit our logic against our experience so we'll have to choose
> between scientific laws and supernatural faith.[15]

In these days (as always), he's looking for those who are more committed to him than to their own understanding.

In this book, I'll be arguing for a change in the evangelical perspective in several areas. Specifically, we need:

+ *A more textured, multilayered view of the Bible.* The people in Scripture were real people with real struggles and real questions about God's will. They didn't know at the time how their story would turn out, and many of them wondered if God would really vindicate their faith. Some, like John the Baptist sitting in prison while Jesus preached about setting captives free, seemed to wrestle with the idea that they had missed God's voice and gotten themselves too far out on a limb.[16] We have to read their stories with these things in mind. Their lives are more textured than we think, with a lot of dynamics and influences and second-guessing going on around them. Their actions and attitudes are also much more layered than we think; in addition to the obvious surface meanings, they're often filled with deeper, symbolic, spiritual significance.

Where we see our Scripture in black and white, we need to start seeing it in color. It isn't a two-dimensional text, it's a multidimensional image. The difference between the way we read it and the images it portrays is stark. We listen to its words like we're listening to a single-speaker radio when, in reality, we should be absorbing it as if we were in the presence of a full orchestra. Otherwise, we'll become very frustrated with our faith when life doesn't fit our one-track expectations.

+ *A willingness to answer theological questions with "I don't know" and not really be bothered that we don't have it figured out.* There's no biblical imperative to fit everything into a systematic theology and force it to make sense. There's no law saying that God must fit into the logic of a Western, modern (or postmodern) worldview. He has not obligated himself to be explainable in terms that a finite mind can sort out. Neither has he obligated his people to be explainable to fellow believers. Accountable, yes. Predictable, no.

+ *A gentler apologetic toward fellow Christians who don't have the same doctrinal positions we do.* There are essentials, of course: the nature of God as a triune being (including the deity of Jesus); the nature of salvation as a gift received by grace through faith in the death and resurrection of Christ; and the inspiration and authority of Scripture. In broad strokes, those are the core beliefs of our faith that can never be compromised. But there's no need to be abrasive about the nonessentials or to label people who love God within those core beliefs as "heretics," as many are prone to do.

+ *An open mind toward the fascinating ways God is moving in our generation.* This is really the main purpose of the book. As I've explained, I believe from what I've observed that we are in an era of the unexpected, a time in which God's Spirit is moving through his people in remarkable ways. If our expectations of how he works are rigid, we'll miss him in the same way that the devout religious leaders missed Jesus. Like Christians in any era, if we don't have a vision of what the Spirit is doing at a big-picture level, we risk falling short of his purpose for our individual lives.[17] It's entirely possible for us to be saved but unfruitful, or at least on the outer fringes of God's most fruitful fields. An overly critical, faultfinding approach that jumps on any variation from traditional understanding or methods will put many in that marginal place, or sometimes even in the unfortunate position of opposing God's work. We do have to be discerning about counterfeits, but we also have to be open to God's unpredictability. That's why a real, intimate, dynamic relationship with him is essential. If we're operating strictly on biblically derived principles rather than with the living Word— a difference we'll explore as we proceed—our discernment won't be accurate. We'll throw the genuine out with the counterfeit and miss God.

Perhaps the best way to address some of our assumptions and refocus on the true nature of God is to take another look at the people he has used throughout history. Imagine the words of ancient Scripture being spoken in our midst today by people who don't have silk robes or halos—regular people with personality quirks and occasional body odor, the kind we might or might not be able to have a decent conversation with if they sat next to us on a bus. The very same words God spoke long ago would be roundly rejected if the very same people spoke them to us today, even if they put them into our cultural context. And we'd have plenty of advice for all of them because we have plenty of "biblical" advice for *everyone.*

In the following pages, we'll explore many of these issues by looking at this overarching question: How would Christians today respond to biblical heroes if they walked into our lives and our churches? What advice would we come up with to try to fix Abraham? What would we say to Ezekiel? How would we counsel Paul? What reactions would we have if we saw and heard Jesus without two thousand years' worth of theology coloring our perspective?

Let me acknowledge up front the challenges of bringing biblical characters into a modern context. Obviously these hypothetical case studies contain anachronisms and a few added peripheral details. After all, we don't always know exactly what these heroes were thinking or how, in light of cultural practices of their day, their behavior would have been received by others.

However, the essence of each character's story has been retained. Bringing their stories into the present illuminates the many unconventional ways in which God works—often through unconventional people. The point is not to tear down what we believe, but to highlight those areas in which we've let rigid yet unbiblical convictions blind us to some of the unpredictable ways God works. I believe that in many respects we've missed his heart because we've been too dogmatic with our own reasoning. In some cases, as we'll see, we've developed even higher standards than the Bible lays out for us. And in the process, we've opposed some things God has wanted to do among us and argued against truths he has wanted to teach us. My hope is that this will change—that as we see how easy it is to fall into the trap of trying to "fix" Abraham and many other servants of God in these illustrations, we'll go a long way toward fixing ourselves.

> *The very same words God spoke long ago would be roundly rejected if the very same people spoke them to us today.*

# THAT SOUNDS DECEPTIVE

"NO," SHEMUEL KEPT TELLING HIMSELF. "I *won't* be deceived. I *won't* disobey. I *won't* neglect the law. I've bound the words of the Lord (blessed be his name) to my hand and my forehead. I've hidden them in my heart. They're on my doorposts. I won't fall for lies. I just *won't*. The Lord (blessed be his name) will keep me in truth."

That wasn't an unusual attitude for a Jew in the time of Jesus. The raw determination to rigidly follow the law and the prophets was one of that era's most admirable characteristics. It's reflected in the Pharisees and priests who, for the most part, were honest, faithful followers of the Torah handed down to them from the time of Moses. Neglecting that law had gotten them in plenty of trouble in the past—a long exile in Babylon, for one example—and it was now the only thing that kept them from assimilating into Greco-Roman society. Stubborn adherence to the revealed will of God was paramount.

It still is. Scripture tells us not to be carried away by every wind of doctrine and to stay away from empty philosophies and arguments. Our potential for being deceived is made abundantly clear in God's Word, so we are rightly zealous about guarding ourselves from falsehood and training ourselves in truth. Discernment is a vital aspect of being a Christian.

But what if our discernment is based on the wrong criteria? What if, like the religious leaders of first-century Judea, our zeal for the details of Scripture causes us to miss the big picture? What if our theological arguments have become the very kind of deceptive talk we're trying to avoid?

That can happen when a relationship with God turns into only a religion about God. It's a very subtle temptation, a constant urge to nail down scriptural parameters that, in all likelihood, don't take into account the whole of Scripture. But we do it. We've all done it. And in the process, we've become so discerning about God's patterns that we miss his peculiarities. The standards of our discernment don't always line up with the standards he applied to people in the Bible—and they aren't the product of living in his presence. The result is that God's voice sometimes sounds deceptive to our ears.

+ + + +

# CHAPTER 1

# CREATIVE INTERPRETATION

*Transcript of NT101 lecture/session 6, Dr. Ferris E. Didaski, professor of biblical hermeneutics, Theologicus Institute of Religion, June 6*

All right, folks, let's get started. You'll notice from your syllabus that we'll be talking about foundational hermeneutic approaches the next couple of weeks, and the reason for this emphasis is the absolutely critical need in our ministries, especially in our preaching, to get the right message from the biblical text. I won't bore you today with endless examples of how the Bible has been misinterpreted and misapplied because you can come up with quite a few examples off the top of your head, I imagine. You've probably heard Aunt Mabel's philosophy on sparing the rod or Brother Jim's earnest desire just to lift Jesus up in worship so all will be drawn to him as he ignores, of course, the plain interpretation that John spells out for us in that text.[1] In one of your outside reading assignments, which we'll probably discuss next time we meet, we find quite a few examples of this kind of misinterpretation, proving that spurious biblical hermeneutics have a long history of abuse and distortion. I want to open your eyes to this—to tear down what you think you know about how the Bible came to us and reconstruct for you a more realistic approach.

Remember rule number one. Don't ever forget this, as long as you live—or at least as long as you preach or teach classes or write articles. Rule number one is "context." The context is the key to understanding any passage. If you miss the original intent of the author in the context in which he wrote, you will find your doctrine corrupted with all sorts of misunderstandings. That is why this class will focus so intensely on the background of the biblical text. You may wish at times that you could just get to the meat of the passage itself, but you will find in the long run that understanding the context in which these sacred Scriptures were written will save you from error. We don't want any false doctrine springing out of this group down the road, do we? So remember, context. Context, context, context.

Now in order to understand the context, you'll need to have a firm grasp of the original language—that's why most of you are muddling through Greek or Hebrew 101 this semester and hating it. Consider it an investment in your commitment to orthodoxy. You'll also need a clear understanding of the history and the cultural and social dynamics of the time, and a very objective approach. These sacred writers did not write in a vacuum, as most people sitting in the pew might imagine. They had their own biases, their own perceptions and observations, and a wide range of influences bearing down on them and coloring the lenses through which they looked. They may have been quite subjective—in fact, they certainly were, without exception. But you are not afforded that privilege.

You must train yourself not to do as they did because they have the authority of apostleship and inspiration behind them and you do not. Adding your subjectivity to theirs will only take you further off course. You must become a Sherlock Holmes of sorts and investigate exactly what the author meant and how his readers understood it. That, my dear students, is how you may become a scholar and a sage instead of a seller of shallow sentiments. The church has too many of the latter. Now, where was I heading with that point . . . oh, yes. The reading. Interestingly, Matthew's Gospel aptly illustrates the hermeneutics we are trying to avoid. But never forget: his writing of the Gospel was inspired. Your interpretation of it is not. Remember that, for as you read it, I want you to see how many misapplications of Scripture you can find. This document will quote extensively from the Hebrew Scriptures, but if you're familiar with said Scriptures, you'll hardly recognize them. I'll give you a few examples to get you started. For instance, there's a prophecy in the book of Isaiah in which God tells the prophet that he will preach to a people who will hear but not understand, and see but not perceive[2]—a prediction that was rather unambiguously fulfilled during the course of Isaiah's ministry. Yet roughly seven centuries later the writer of this document quotes this passage and says "now it is being fulfilled" in his own day.[3] Or, for one a little more egregious, a Hosea passage clearly referring to Israel's exodus from Egypt[4] is applied to the Messiah figure[5] as though the primary meaning of the prophecy had never even occurred to the writer.

This is clearly not proof of the Messiah, though the writer evidently thinks it is. And again, Micah's assessment of the Israelites' lamentable condition in his own day is used by Matthew to depict how the Messiah would pull families apart![6] Or, if you need more to go on, a passage in Jeremiah about the Babylonian captivity is applied to the children of Bethlehem centuries later.[7] We even have one example where the scribe quotes a verse in Jeremiah about thirty pieces of silver, not noticing that this passage occurs nowhere in Jeremiah but in Zechariah instead.[8] This list could go on and on, of course, but that's for you to discover as you read.

I hate to cast aspersions on our most revered New Testament writer, but Paul appears guilty of careless interpretation at times as well. You may recall Romans 1:17, the verse that, in some degree, launched the Reformation: "the righteous will live by faith" (NIV). Now what does that mean, do you suppose? It could mean that those who are righteous will live in a faithful way; or that those who are righteous came to be so because of their faithful living; or that the just shall survive, i.e., not be condemned, because of their faith; or so on. And, in fact, when we turn to the original passage, Habakkuk 2:4, it seems more likely that the prophet intended to say that those who are righteous will live in a faithful manner. But Paul seems to apply the verse to matters of final judgment or present justification; and Martin Luther certainly understood the verse this way, crediting it with opening his eyes to the doctrine of justification by faith alone. The question I would pose to you, and which we will discuss on Thursday, is that as this truth is being bounced around like a beach ball, who blew it up to begin with? Obviously, Habakkuk did. So we should rightly defer to his intentions for the right interpretation. This will be our guiding principle in this course and, I hope, yours for the rest of your life.

Now, let's turn our attention to the related matter of exegesis—drawing truth out of the original text—as opposed to the scandal of *eis*egesis—by which we mean reading our own interpretations into the text. . . .

++++

I recently heard a well-known Bible teacher lecturing about hermeneutics—one's method of interpreting the Bible—on the radio. He opened his talk with an illustration of a former student of his, a young woman who was in zealous pursuit of a husband. Not a particular husband, just a husband. As I recall the story, she had recently broken up with a man and was feeling rather despondent over her prospects. But one day she came to this professor with a bright smile on her face, declaring in all sincerity that she was soon going to meet her husband and get married. How did she know this? the professor asked. She had indulged in "lucky dipping" the night before, she explained. That was her term for the practice of opening up the Bible and reading the verse your finger lands on, hoping that it's God's word to you for the moment. She didn't normally do this, she said, but she felt inspired to do so that evening, and the results were very encouraging. Whatever verse she landed on, it resonated with her, telling her that her desire would be fulfilled shortly and that it would even happen within a couple of weeks.[9] She was convinced the Spirit had told her that it was a promise from God.

For obvious reasons, the professor was amused at the attempt. That's not a very scholarly approach to Scripture. So as he was finishing describing this negative example on the radio program, he introduced his topic for the day: keys to biblical interpretation. And he almost got fully into the "right" way to study Scripture without mentioning the end of the story, but he couldn't resist. "Now as it turns out," he said (and I'm paraphrasing), "she did happen to meet a man a couple of weeks later and they ended up getting married. I keep in touch with them to this day. But I tell her that God did that in spite of her faulty hermeneutic rather than because of it!" And he laughed.

No offense to this respected Bible scholar, but that's the worst possible illustration he could have used to introduce his point. I have no idea whether that girl's promise from God actually came from God, but I suspect that in her situation it did. Would I recommend "lucky dipping" as a regular practice? Obviously not. But neither would I say God never works that way. In this case, he apparently did; what she believed did happen, down to the specific detail. But because this preacher's theology couldn't bend to that possibility, he believed it happened "in spite of" her superstitious approach to God's Word.

I've read, heard, and participated in numerous doctrinal discussions in which a phrase like "That's not what that verse means!" or "That's taken out of context" occurs. That's because we have essentially one approach to biblical interpretation: that of the professor in the fictitious lecture transcript above.

We can always stop a heresy in its tracks by appealing to "original context" or the "original language," as well as to our principles of logic. But in doing so, we're basically undermining the many ways the writers of the New Testament employed Hebrew Scripture in their Gospels and letters. If we held people like Matthew to our hermeneutical standards, he would be laughed out of any respectable seminary today. Those verses pulled from the Old Testament would be "proven" to have little to do with the Messiah and therefore not applicable to Jesus through any reasonable method of interpretation. Yet Matthew was inspired by the Holy Spirit to write those things. His hermeneutic was apparently acceptable to God.

How can this be? Why would God authorize bypassing the plain meaning of a verse and using it in a secondary or even symbolic sense that had little to do with the original context? One answer lies in normal biblical interpretation at the time the New Testament was written. Rabbinic interpreters from ages past used four main interpretive methods for understanding Jewish Scriptures. The first was *p'shat*: the literal meaning of a text, the plain and simple objective facts. That was the primary hermeneutic then, and it's still our default hermeneutic. It's foundational for developing doctrine and should form the backbone of all other interpretations. But with the Jewish sages, unlike with us, it didn't end there. The second means of interpretation was the *remez*: the deeper meaning hinted at in the subtleties and nuances of the text. Third was the *drash* or *midrash*: the comparative, allegorical, metaphorical meaning drawn from the verse as it related to others using similar symbolism or terminology or even word forms. And then there was the *sod*: the hidden meaning, the philosophical meanderings prompted by the text, the secret or mystical interpretation. It was very subjective and, though acceptable during certain periods of Christian history, has remained very unwelcome in Christian interpretation for the last few centuries.[10]

I've heard seminary professors and well-known pastors issue strict warnings against looking for some passage's "hidden meaning." But New Testament writers and early Christians relied on *sod* sometimes.[11] All four modes of interpretation came into play, and there was nothing contemptible about any of them. You wouldn't build doctrine on the more mystical interpretations, obviously, but you wouldn't ignore them either. They would supplement your faith and inform your more objective interpretations. All were fair game.

This puts us in a difficult spot. Today we have a hermeneutic that forbids the kind of hermeneutic used by the inspired writers of the Old and New Testament and even by Jesus himself.[12] In other words, our limited mode of interpretation doesn't match God's broader intentions for his Word. To me, that sounds like a pretty indefensible position.

Our rigid interpretations have led to some pretty harsh criticisms of people who quote the Bible or explain how God spoke to them through his Word. If those people don't quote the verse with the exact meaning and original context in mind, a chorus of accusations arises: that person must be "ignorant," "unbiblical," or even "heretical." No other symbolic or imaginative interpretation is allowed, no hints and subtleties, no intuitive impressions—nothing but clear, objective fact. Some of the words I used in the previous sentence would be extremely alarming to many biblical scholars and Christian teachers and apologists, but that's only because we forbid hermeneutical approaches that the Bible itself allows. That's an odd position to be in, isn't it? In our zeal to be biblical, we've become decidedly unbiblical.

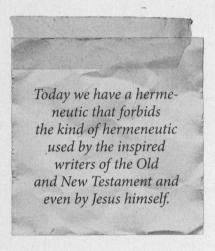

*Today we have a hermeneutic that forbids the kind of hermeneutic used by the inspired writers of the Old and New Testament and even by Jesus himself.*

Obviously, I have no reason to criticize Christian versions of *p'shat* and *remez*. I think the objective, contextual approach to Scripture is vital. This is where we get the plain meaning of God's Word and discover the truth about God's attributes and the plan of salvation and all sorts of doctrinal essentials.

But this kind of interpretation will never give specific guidance in specific situations not covered in Scripture. I was once profoundly encouraged and filled with faith when the words of a passage jumped out at me. It was a passage making a spiritual application from an agricultural principle, and when it mentioned "rain," I knew what it meant symbolically for my situation, even though my situation didn't really fit the original context. The Holy Spirit spoke at that moment—and on countless other occasions since—by taking a phrase or metaphor in Scripture out of its immediate context and applying it to my personal issues. This happens quite often in personal guidance, as well as in broader biblical interpretation when the Spirit unfolds layers of his truth.

For example, depending on what you're going through and how the Spirit has been working in your life, the statement that "No eye has seen, no ear has heard, no mind has conceived what God has prepared for those who love him" (1 Corinthians 2:9, NIV) can mean different things. To someone at a funeral, it speaks of promises of eternal glory. To someone making a decision about a career or a mate, the Spirit can use it for reassurance of God's good plans for us in this age. To those going through a spiritual awakening, the Spirit may inspire a vision for going well beyond the "normal" or "status quo" Christianity that most people experience. And what did it mean in the original context? Well, that depends on which "original context" you're talking about. Paul was referring to God's revelation of his deep, mysterious wisdom—the plan of the ages—through the nascent church. But Paul was actually quoting Isaiah, who had been inspired to write this statement about how God acts on behalf of those who wait for him.[13] One inspired statement, multiple inspired interpretations and applications—some of them not even hinted at until hundreds of years later. That's what it means to read the living Word.

This idea makes a lot of people nervous, and there's certainly some basis for that. Scripture has been distorted and manipulated, used for evil purposes, or simply misunderstood by noninspired interpreters. Cults have sprung up from a few twistings of Scripture for selfish or ungodly purposes. But it grates against my understanding and experience of who God is to believe that people who are humbly seeking truth and asking the Holy Spirit to guide them while affirming a willingness to be corrected by other parts of Scripture will make such an error. It's generally pride or an underlying agenda, not a faulty hermeneutic, that leads people to false interpretations of the Word. In fact, I'd argue that humble interaction with the Spirit is much more likely to lead someone into truth than strictly logical study of Scripture would.

The most common biblical objection to approaching Scripture as the Living Word is 2 Peter 1:20: "No prophecy of Scripture is a matter of one's own interpretation." But no one in rabbinic circles of long ago or in the church today, as far as I know—there are always fringe exceptions—would say that this fourfold approach to interpretation falls in that category of self-interpretation. Just as the Holy Spirit inspired people to write the words of Scripture, he opens the reader's ears to hear what he wants them to hear. He is intricately involved in the interpretation, just as he was in the inspiration. If we say one end of that process is reliable and the other isn't, we have a pretty strange doctrine of the Holy Spirit. The fact that the Bible is his own breath during any moment when it is being written or read opens the door for hearing the Spirit in full and exciting ways.

*Your interactions with the Spirit will go in directions that never contradict the Word but often expand your understanding of it, even uncomfortably at times.*

I'm a huge proponent of intellectual understanding, but experiencing God is not simply a matter of knowing biblical truth. The Bible is much, much more than a sourcebook for divine principles. When read by someone in fellowship with the Spirit who authored it, it becomes a living, breathing companion that may surprise you at some point in the conversation. It's interactive, inviting you to ask questions and hear answers not only about doctrine but about what, specifically, to do with your life the next couple of years or whom to associate with. And it's the *beginning* of the conversation, not the definition of it. Your interactions with the Spirit will go in directions that never contradict the Word but often expand your understanding of it, even uncomfortably at times.

I have several friends, for example, who have wrestled with their experiences at worship services that seemed very disorderly, which, in their understanding, violated 1 Corinthians 14:33 and 40: "God is not a God of disorder but of peace. . . . Everything should be done in a fitting and orderly way" (NIV). This struggle is common to visitors at an Orthodox church, a charismatic church, and everything in between. Why? Because what's orderly to one person isn't necessarily orderly to another. Members of highly liturgical churches often find Baptist and Methodist services much too casual and disorganized, while Baptists and Methodists can make little sense of a Catholic service on the first few visits. Orthodox services have no concrete beginning or end, and a standing and pacing congregation seems at times to be rather detached from the priestly duties being carried out. And charismatic worship services are seen by many as a free-for-all. Any of the above can be a violation of "fitting and orderly" by someone's standards because order is in the eye of the beholder.

In every one of these cases, however, those who have been immersed in the "culture" of the given church can easily see the parameters and predictability in their own worship services. In each flavor of Christian expression, there's a sense of what's appropriate and what isn't, of the right and wrong times for whatever takes place, of doing things in their proper order. But a rigid definition of Paul's instructions about "fitting and orderly"—a definition that a person most often equates with his or her own upbringing—might keep a person away from a fellowship the Holy Spirit is guiding him or her to become involved in. The Spirit is under no obligation to comply with our expectations.[14]

Yet reading the Bible as a living, dynamic, organic voice makes people afraid. It just opens it up to all kinds of misinterpretation, some say—as though the purely objective, contextual hermeneutic has led everyone to the same conclusions. Regardless of the interpretive approach, the Spirit is a necessary companion. When he's ignored, misinterpretation is likely. But when he's involved, God speaks. Is that infallible? Nope. But neither is anyone else's hermeneutic. And I'd rather walk hand in hand with the Spirit through Scripture than trust my objective reasoning alone.

I find it rather liberating to know that my interpretation of a passage of Scripture isn't necessarily *my* interpretation—that the Holy Spirit is stirring up within me an understanding that he has long desired to impart to

*Whenever the Spirit is ignored, misinterpretation is likely. But whenever he's involved, God speaks.*

me and anyone else who will listen to him carefully. Are there dangers in my belief that he speaks hidden meanings? Of course—there are dangers in *any* kind of interpretation of Scripture. But I know from the overt, literal meaning of Scripture what his character is like and how he works, so that's a guardrail of sorts. He won't violate that. So if I tell him that I'm trusting him to speak in a way I understand and to keep me from error, I can be confident that he'll do that. When I (or any other Christian) ask the Spirit to unfold his truth—and to guard my heart and mind from error—hints and parallels and images seem to come to mind much more often. These, in turn, can be sifted through and examined in the light of the rest of Scripture just as any sermon or book would be. But almost always, such interpretations deepen one's understanding of the Bible and offer guidance in current circumstances. Why? Because just as the Spirit was in the hands of the writers who penned Scripture, he's in the hearts of those reading it.

*Just as the Spirit was in the hand of the writers who penned Scripture, he's in the heart that's reading it.*

I have a recurring mental picture of evangelicalism's doctrinal guardians criticizing someone—let's say me, for example, since that's usually who's in my picture—applying a verse in a way that's unconventional and doesn't pay enough homage to the original context. Charges of "mysticism" and "distorting God's Word" and "ignoring the plain meaning of the text" are flying all over the place. Then I envision Matthew walking over to me and saying, "Why are they so mad at us?" And I answer, "Me, because I heard God say something. You, because you misused the Bible when you wrote the Bible." And then we get into a discussion of the irony of an "unbiblical" hermeneutic becoming biblical by authenticating itself within the pages of Scripture.

I'm strongly convinced that there's nothing in Matthew's interpretation of Scripture that needs to be fixed. I love studying the original context and languages of the Bible, and I do it almost obsessively. But there are other ways—intuitive, philosophical, mystical, metaphorical, etc.—

of hearing God's voice in the Word. Really all it takes is to ask him and be open to how he leads and reveals himself and his Word. There are no special techniques, no formulas, no step-by-step instructions. Just ask. And expect. And if it's still uncertain, ask him about your uncertainties. The Holy Spirit was there at the inspiration of Scripture, he has preserved it over the centuries, he has opened countless minds and hearts to its truth, and he's right there with you as you read it, discern it, and discover new aspects to it.

But opening ourselves up to more layers of meaning requires loosening our exclusive grip on the ones we already know. If we want to have more intimate fellowship with him, we'll need to learn how to hear him unconventionally. Not unbiblically, mind you, but unexpectedly and unashamedly. And always true to who he is.

**FORGOTTEN LESSONS FROM MATTHEW:**
+ The Bible is alive, constantly moving and breathing into us— and the Spirit can speak through it however he chooses.
+ Today's rigid hermeneutic is only part of true biblical interpretation. By itself, it's insufficient for hearing and understanding God's voice as a means of specific guidance in a personal conversation with him.
+ The Spirit was there when the Bible was inspired, and he's there when we read it. It's okay to trust him with the text.

# CHAPTER 2

# THE MOSTLY TRUE PROPHET

"Welcome to the Dr. Discernment Show. I'm your host, Dr. Phil Logo-machia, and I'll be here for the next couple of hours to answer your questions about the Bible. So let's get right to it, shall we? Steve, you're our first caller today. What's your question for Dr. Discernment?"

"Hey, Doc, love the show, man. Thanks for taking my call. I've been listening for years, and you've really helped me out a lot. I can't believe I'm actually talking to you."

"My pleasure, Steve. Thanks for listening. What's on your mind?"

"Well, it's that guy on the news last night. I forget his name . . . you know, he's been around for years, says he's a prophet and was talking about how this country's headed for disaster and—"

"An invasion's coming, the end is near, it's just a matter of time, blah, blah, blah. Yeah, I know. Not real original. Somebody needs to tell the man the sixties ended decades ago."

"I mean, it's not like anybody takes him seriously—I'm not worried about that. But I just want to be able to say . . . like, when people are laughing about him at work, I want to know how to respond biblically to that kind of stuff. 'Cause, you know, that's what a lot of people think of when they think of Christians. Like we're all whacked-out that way."

"Okay, well, there are several ways to do this, Steve. We can expose him from any number of angles. Let's start with his 'prophecies'—and I use that term loosely, of course, because the guy's definitely not a prophet. This is what people don't understand about prophecy, and why you can't just go throwing that term around like so many people do today. In the Bible, a true prophet is accurate 100 percent of the time. If he's wrong, even a small percentage of the time, he's a false prophet. That's in Deuteronomy 18:20-22. And, of course, the Israelites had the death penalty for that, which kind of inhibited people from claiming to 'have a word from the Lord' all the time. They stoned you if it didn't come true. Sometimes I think that wouldn't necessarily be a bad policy today, you know?"

"Yeah, seriously!"

"Just kidding, of course. So this 'prophet' you're talking about, look at his track record. He gets away with this stuff because people have short memories, but clearly he's been wrong before. You remember when the president was sick a few years ago? This guy prophesied not just that he would die, but that he would die from that particular illness. Now it's years later, and Mr. President's walking around in perfect health. So right there, that's enough to call him a false prophet."

"Okay, but what if, like, the circumstances changed after he prophesied . . . like maybe the president prayed or repented, or something like that?"

"Doesn't matter. That's not what he predicted. He didn't say, 'Unless you repent, you'll die.' He simply said, 'You aren't going to get well. You're going to die.' And he was pretty emphatic about it. No loopholes. So there you have it. False prophet. End of story."

"Yeah, that's true. The way he said it was sort of unconditional."

"Right. That was unusual, and I don't think he'll try it again. Most of his prophecies now are so vague and so far in the future that there's no way to prove whether he's right or not. Pretty convenient, huh? That's what most of these people do. Instead of predicting something that will happen soon, something objective that will clearly show whether they're right or wrong, they usually talk about things that won't happen in our lifetime, or that are so symbolic that almost any event could be said to fulfill them. And you see why, right? When this guy predicted the imminent death of our country's leader, it became obvious real quick that he had no idea what he was talking about."

"Yeah, that's true. But he says a lot of things that are right on target, though. I mean, he quotes the Bible a lot."

"Of course he does. That's how Satan deceives people—a lot of truth with just the right amount of error thrown in. Remember, counterfeits are supposed to look like the real thing. But Jesus said we'll know a tree by its fruit, so quoting the Bible doesn't really mean anything. Pay attention to this man's life, not his words. His life doesn't line up with the Word of God. He's got a long, flaky history that a lot of people don't know about. For starters, even though he says he's a 'minister,' he doesn't actually have a ministry. No church will hire him. He *was* ordained years ago—I think he comes from a pretty respected family in ministry, actually—and I think he served in a church somewhere. But then he had some 'vision' that, frankly, turned a lot of people off. When you start telling people you visited God's throne room and received a special assignment from the Almighty, that's pretty arrogant, and most people are able to see right through it. But it gets a lot of attention, which I guess is what that kind of person wants. Then people who are ignorant of the Bible and who are impressed with sensationalism jump on the bandwagon. But there are better ways to resurrect a dying ministry. Certainly more godly ways. This is what happens when people start basing their lives on an alleged 'experience' rather than on the Word of God itself. They get further and further off track. And so do their followers. Trusting someone else's mystical experience is a dangerous place to be."

"Do you think he really could have had a vision?"

"Please. Like I said, if someone had a vision like that, which wouldn't happen now since the Bible is complete, his life would show genuine fruit. What's this guy got to show for it? No one really takes him seriously—I mean no one who's well educated and has even a hint of common sense—and he can't hold down a job. He's basically an entertainer. Whatever gets attention, that's what he does. You'll notice that as much as he *talks* about God, most of what he *does* draws attention to himself. Always watch for that."

"Yeah, actions speak louder than words."

"And you know who I really feel sorry for, Steve? His children. Instead of names, they have political labels because he wanted to make a statement when they were born. So they have to live with that stigma their whole lives . . . or else change their names, which is probably what I'd do as soon as I got old enough. And then there was 'the episode.' Seriously, who walks around naked for three years to make a point—*and* expects anyone to actually believe God told him to do that? Does that sound like something God would say? That just isn't how he works, obviously. If you want to make a statement about our international allies, then give a speech or write an editorial or something. You don't have to be so dramatic . . . or indecent, for that matter. So that was hugely embarrassing for him and for the administration—and really for all Christians, because like you said, that's how a lot of people perceive us."

"I know, and that's what drives me nuts. That's what people see because that's what the media talks about. And then the rest of us, the vast majority of Christians who are trying to be good examples, get stuck with that stereotype."

"Yep, that's exactly right. And don't underestimate the political damage he's done either. The *last* thing the administration needs right now is some high-profile circus clown criticizing our international diplomacy with sound bites and headlines. He has absolutely no background in foreign affairs, but for some reason he thinks he can give advice to people who are a lot more educated about it than he is. That's not a real godly thing to do. So that says a lot about where this guy's coming from. He isn't a real godly kind of guy."

"So when I'm talking to people about him, which of those things should I start with?"

"I'd start with the fact that most of his prophecies have either been proven wrong or are so far in the future that no one will ever know if they were true or not. But point out his behavior too. Remind them that he's been almost universally rejected by informed religious leaders, tell them that real Christians would never engage in public indecency like he has, even tell them what his kids are named—I'm sure they'll find that interesting. The best way to be a witness in that situation is just to show that real Christians are coming from a whole different place. It doesn't matter that some of what he says sounds biblical, when you consider the total package, it's obvious he's not speaking for God—or for us. He's a nutcase."

"Okay, Doc, thanks for your time. That helps a lot."

"No problem, Steve. Thanks for calling the *Dr. Discernment Show*. Wow, what a crazy world we live in, folks. I guess that's why I'm in this business. All right, let's take another caller...."

+ + + +

Isaiah is probably the most widely read and respected prophet in the Bible, both in Jewish and Christian circles. In his book we find astounding prophecies of the Messiah and ultimate prophecies of the coming Kingdom. We learn that a virgin will conceive, that a suffering servant will bear our sins, that the Anointed One will preach good news to the poor and freedom for captives, that his name will mean "God with us," and that the wolf and the lamb will eat together in peace. Isaiah's dramatic vision in which he received his calling has become the source of countless sermons and hymns, to the point that we can almost see the train of the Lord's robe in the Temple and hear the angels shouting "Holy, holy, holy, is the Lord Almighty." The majestic and sweeping words of this prolific prophet are inspiring.[1]

Have you ever considered how we'd respond to Isaiah today? I've tried to imagine that, and the result isn't very encouraging. (See the fictional radio transcript above, for one example.) I'm pretty sure the church would be full of critics and counselors—critics to point out all his imprecise doctrine and unconventional methods, and counselors to advise him against some of the things he experienced and taught.[2] In fact, I think if we really broke down Isaiah's ministry into pieces, we'd find quite a few unacceptable themes. For example, what would we say about these?

+ Saying his words are God's words. We might say: "That's pretty nervy, telling everyone that your opinions are what 'God says.' Who elected you his special confidant? We all have a relationship with God too. Don't you think if he wanted to tell us something, he'd tell us directly?"[3]

+ His distant prophecies. "Predicting events hundreds of years in advance is pointless. No one can validate your prophecies, and they certainly aren't going to benefit any of us. By the time the world gets there, no one's going to remember what you've written anyway. Besides, you have to be really vague about things that far in the future—which means your predictions can be interpreted to fit just about anything."[4]

+ His behavior. "God told you to go naked for three years? Now let's think this one through: does that *sound* like something God would say? Can you see that as something that would bring him any honor at all? Or do you think maybe another voice is trying to deceive you—and dishonor God in the process?[5] And who names their kid 'Maher-shalal-hash-baz'? He'll never live it down: 'quick to the spoil, fast to the prey.' Poor kid."[6]

+ His unfulfilled prophecy about Hezekiah. "Don't be so fast next time to say that's God's voice that you heard. See how quickly you had to backtrack? If you were really speaking for God, you wouldn't contradict yourself like that. God isn't wrong. That was you."[7]

+ His vision and calling. "Doesn't it seem a little presumptuous to claim you were in God's throne room? And that he gave you a special mission? And you know, you don't really help your case with that disclaimer that God said people wouldn't actually heed your words or recognize them as God's. That just sounds like an excuse to justify in advance why you've failed."[8]

+ His wide prophetic extremes. "You're always either preaching doom and gloom real soon or gazing into the future with Pollyanna eyes. There's nothing in between. I find it hard to believe things will be as bad as you say or as great as you say. That's too shallow. Real life is somewhere in the middle. Not total disaster, not pie in the sky. People aren't looking for over-simplified, black-and-white answers."[9]

+ His political meddling. "And what experience in foreign affairs did you say you had? Oh, none at all? Really? Then keep your unpatriotic mouth shut! You're not helping our leaders when you expose the division in our country while we're trying to present a unified front to Egypt. Same goes for your military 'advice.' Button it up. You obviously know nothing of Assyrian war tactics. And your transparent support for Babylon is downright treasonous. You're practically begging them to invade."[10]

This speculation may seem merely hypothetical, but the fact is that this prophet universally loved by Jews and Christians today was, in reality, not broadly accepted in his day. He had the ear of kings, but other than Hezekiah most of them ignored his advice. As the country hurtled toward judgment, he continued to preach an unpopular message. As is the case with artists—they're usually only appreciated after they're dead—prophets like Isaiah were rejected for speaking the very words of God until decades or even centuries later. So we know that such elegant and literary prophecies don't always appear that way in the prophet's own generation.

But we somehow seem to think we'd be different—that if biblical prophets walked into our lives today, our biblical worldview would lead us to accept them as brothers in faith. That's foolish. For reasons cited above, we'd reject people like Isaiah. And, for those reasons, we should be extremely wary when we find ourselves rejecting someone who is speaking in the name of the Lord. We have to remember that if it really is God's voice, most people attached to the status quo will reject it.[11] That has always been the case, and it always will be. Public outcry alone, even from highly educated and respected scholars and ministers, is no indication of whether someone has a message from God or not.

That was pretty obvious in Jesus' ministry. "Woe to you," he warned the religious leaders, "because you build tombs for the prophets, and it was your forefathers who killed them" (Luke 11:47, NIV). Or to paraphrase, "Why do you claim the prophets as your heroes? Your own ancestors were the ones who killed them!" That's because prophets are only honored when there's enough time and/or distance between us and them;[12] in the present, they just get on our nerves.

*Prophets are only honored when there's enough time and distance between us and them; in the present, they just get on our nerves.*

So who in our religious circles today gets on your nerves? Who's out there embarrassing the rest of us Christians? Who's meddling in national or international matters in which they have no expertise? What Christian leaders seem too divisive and controversial to be sent from God?

Whoever you identify as fitting the above criteria may or may not be a genuine servant of God. These characteristics don't prove anything. Not everyone who's embarrassing, meddling, and divisive is from God. (In fact, quite a few are not.) Even our old reliable interpretation of Deuteronomy's definition of a true prophet isn't quite as reliable as we thought it was. Not only would we reject Isaiah because of its surface premise, we'd also reject Jonah. He told the Ninevites that in forty days they would be overthrown,[13] no ifs, ands, or buts. Forty days passed, and they weren't overthrown. Anyone with knowledge of the Scripture would be able to identify Jonah as a false prophet. Yet we now know what happened in heavenly councils. Nineveh repented, and God turned away his wrath. But the prophecy sure looked like a bust at the time.

The point is that all of the criteria listed on the previous page are not valid for determining whether or not someone has a message from God. There's nothing inherently godly or ungodly about getting on people's nerves, behaving in embarrassing ways, meddling in society's affairs, or being divisive and controversial. Some people fit that criteria perfectly and are charlatans. Isaiah and plenty of other prophets and messengers match that description exactly and are genuine men and women of God on a divine mission.

We have a responsibility to discern the spirit behind certain ministries and secular leaders, but these are not the criteria we can use for our discernment.

If they were, we'd have to rip quite a few pages out of our Bibles. No, the criteria we use involve those foundational doctrines I mentioned on page xxi, whether a person or ministry is self-centered or Christ-centered, how well he/she/it embodies the message of the Cross, and whether the fruit is the kind God grows. If you spend time in the presence of God and ask the Spirit for the mind of Christ, you will, over time, have the discernment you need. But you won't be led to judge a ministry solely on the basis of whether it's unusual, undignified, or controversial.

*You shouldn't judge a ministry solely on the basis of whether it's unusual, undignified, or controversial.*

This is particularly relevant because of the prophetic movement springing up among churches around the world.[14] The practice of prophetic words of encouragement and exhortation has been cultivated in many churches and denominations in response to New Testament passages about the role of prophecy. But many people dismiss the idea that prophecy is a legitimate gift in the church today.[15]

Having studied the many references to this gift in the New Testament[16] and having personally seen it in operation in several churches—people speaking into the lives of others in very specific, personal terms that could only have been revealed by the Spirit, with the result that those who receive such words have been strengthened, encouraged, and comforted according to 1 Corinthians 14:3 (NIV)—I strongly believe in its authenticity. In fact, Paul instructed the Corinthians to "desire earnestly to prophesy" (1 Corinthians 14:39) and commanded the Thessalonians not to despise prophetic utterances,[17] and there's no indication that this practice is limited to a specific era. In fact, in light of the ample New Testament evidence for prophetic proclamations, I think it is negligent and disobedient for the church *not* to recognize this gift today. That said, we can always expect the real and the counterfeit to flow together when God is working—which means we must be discerning. There *are* false prophets out there. But that doesn't mean that the entire prophetic movement is a dangerous departure from orthodox Christianity.

In addition to the prophetic gift of the Spirit, we also have a hard time knowing what to do with prophet-like behavior. I know of a minister who used to preach with a bag over his head so his expressions and identity wouldn't get in the way of his own message. Now that's weird. I think if I were in the congregation, that might actually do more to get in the way of the message. But I'd be way out of line to say that God wouldn't lead him to do something like that. That's *exactly* the kind of thing God inspired his prophets and leaders to do in the pages of Scripture. That kind of action pales in comparison to the extremes Isaiah or Ezekiel might have indulged in to get their message across. That doesn't impress any boards of deacons or elders, and it might keep the big donors away. But what do you think God is more interested in: Radical messages or donor appeal? demonstrative expression or dignified presentations? passionate, reckless worship or following the order in the bulletin down to the minute?

People like Isaiah, no matter how *offbeat*, should be honored in our own generation.

Sadly, the hypothetical radio transcript above is not a far-fetched conversation. It's exactly the kind of discussion that would take place if Isaiah stepped onto the scene today. Most evangelical churches would go out of their way to separate themselves from "that kind of ministry." The more flaky expressions of the Christian faith may make it on TV, but the evangelical community in general creates a certain distance from them because we don't want to be perceived that way. Some of these people may be deviant in their theology or methodology, and others may be entirely legitimate. But "flaky" shouldn't enter into the discussion. Things like integrity, lining up with the character of God, and demonstrating the fruit of the Spirit—accompanied by the discernment of a community that can appraise according to the Spirit rather than the flesh[18]—should carry much more weight than whether or not someone seems "normal." And people like Isaiah, no matter how offbeat, should be honored in our own generation.

## FORGOTTEN MESSAGES FROM ISAIAH:

+ True prophets sometimes say things that appear false, so the definition of a true prophet in Deuteronomy 18:20-22, like much of the law, isn't as unyielding or precise as most people think it is.
+ Controversial behavior is no indication that someone isn't representing God.
+ God sometimes inspires prophecy that isn't testable in its own generation. And he's under no obligation to make his words provable or disprovable by watchdog ministries.
+ It's within the realm of possibility for God to inspire someone— but probably not you—to go naked for three years to make a point.

# CHAPTER 3

# SECONDHAND STORIES

"You're so gullible, Jan. Don't believe everything you hear."

"Well, Bill, at least I have faith. You're so skeptical you wouldn't believe Jesus if he were standing right in front of you."

"That's not true. I believe the miracles in the Bible. I just don't believe what that church is trying to pass off as miracles. It's obvious that some of those healings are staged. Besides, didn't you used to say you married me for my common sense?"

"Yeah. What was I thinking?"

"Ha! You couldn't resist my charms. But then, I used to love how naive you were too."

"Used to?"

"Well, it's still kind of sweet. I just don't want you to fall for what that ministry is selling. They can make 'miracles' look pretty real."

"Have you considered that sometimes maybe they *are* real? I mean, Shauna was there. She saw the guy get up and walk with her own eyes."

"But did she know he was really crippled to begin with? How does she know he wasn't planted in the audience—that he wasn't healthy to start with? Maybe he even travels with that ministry and gets healed in every city."

"Oh, come on, Bill. Don't you think Shauna would be able to tell if it was a setup?"

"Shauna? Oh, yeah, she's real discerning. Didn't she also sign up to sell that miracle skin cream a couple of years ago before she found out it didn't work? Let's see, how much of that 'unlimited income' has her multilevel marketing career earned for her? Yeah, that's who you want to trust."

"I'm not saying she's always right about things. I agree that she can be a little too trusting. But she's not an idiot. She said the healing looked real, and I believe her."

"Jan, that's my point. It *looks* real. It has to look real, otherwise nobody would believe it and they wouldn't be able to keep making money."

"I know there are a lot of scams and counterfeits out there, but I don't think these people are in it for the money, Bill."

"Really? Don't they sell products when they come to a church? Most of those people do. I bet they have a pretty spiffy Web site too—with lots of 'limited time only' offers."

"I wouldn't know about that. I haven't looked. I'm just saying, maybe God heals people sometimes."

"I'm sure he does. All I'm saying is that if it's possible to explain something in natural terms, then that's probably the right explanation. A miracle is when there's no other possible explanation."

"Well, that guy that Shauna saw got up without any explanation."

"No, he didn't. If he wasn't really crippled, there's your explanation."

"Bill, that doesn't make any sense. What if he really was crippled?"

"Well, you can't know that for sure. And that's always how it is. Seems like 'miracles' only happen to people whom nobody knows and whose healings can't be verified later by medical examinations. Very suspicious."

"Okay, then what about our friends who went on that mission trip to Africa a few years ago and saw that little boy raised from the dead? They're from our church, Bill. Our friends. We know them and trust them."

"Oh, no. Not that again. You already know what I think about that. I think they were gullible too. They didn't know that little boy from Adam. Now, do I believe that they believe they saw a real resurrection? Sure. But I think they got caught up in the moment and believed what their hosts said about the boy. They saw what they wanted to see."

"Bill, he was dead. He'd been lying there without breathing for hours."

"Jan, I didn't see it, so I don't trust it. Maybe they have some herbal concoction that makes people look dead. Maybe they found a look-alike boy and took the dead body away when no one was watching. I don't know. But I do know that whenever a story that strange is floating around, it's either greatly exaggerated or there was some natural explanation behind it to begin with. I wouldn't believe something that absurd unless I saw it with my own eyes. And even then I'd be looking for an explanation."

"You wouldn't have made a very good disciple, then."

"Sure I would. Listen, following Jesus doesn't mean turning your brain off. If Jesus did a miracle, I'd believe it—because it's him. But when someone we know in this day and age tells us something like that ... well, I know enough psychology to understand that we believe what we want to believe. Besides, I can't think of any place in the Bible where Jesus told his disciples to believe what somebody else told them they thought they saw. The disciples saw things with their own eyes. And didn't he encourage them to be discerning? And to test the spirits? And to watch out for false teachers? That's all I'm doing. I'm using the brain God gave me."

"And I'm not?"

"Let's just say you forget to ask the right questions sometimes."

+ + + +

Jesus had appeared to Mary Magdalene and at least two of the disciples, but for the others, the good news of his resurrection hadn't sunk in yet. It seemed so fanciful, so unrealistic, so ... outrageously impossible. Surely these "appearances" were the product of wishful thinking or maybe even spiritual visions from God. But a real bodily resurrection? There had to be some other explanation.

The skepticism of the disciples is a lot like our own. In spite of the fact that they had seen plenty of miracles in their three years with Jesus, they still couldn't believe in the resurrection he had foretold until they actually saw him standing before them. So how did Jesus greet their cautious attitude? "He reproached them for their unbelief and hardness of heart, *because they had not believed those who had seen Him* after He had risen" (Mark 16:14, italics added).

Did you catch that? Jesus fully expected his followers to believe an outlandish report about something they hadn't seen for themselves. Why? Because it came from reliable witnesses.

That runs contrary to our usual approach to such things. We're trained from an early age not to be too gullible. "If something seems too good to be true, it probably is," conventional wisdom says. "I won't believe it until I see it," I've said on more than a few occasions. Our general assumption is that no testimony is reliable because people can easily be deceived by outward appearances, trickery, and their own wishful thinking. Our approach is "don't believe it until it's proven true." And this perspective is apparently worthy of Jesus' strong rebuke.

The perspective Jesus really wanted his disciples to have—at least with regard to his own ministry—was to believe now and ask questions later. He often rebuked people for skepticism about miracles, but there's no evidence he rebuked anyone for being too trusting of them.[1] No offense to the fine residents of Missouri, but Jesus didn't come from the "show me" state. He wanted his followers' natural response to his ministry to be "yes, it must be true."

> *Jesus often rebuked people for skepticism about miracles, but there's no evidence he rebuked anyone for being too trusting of them.*

Over the years, I've heard numerous reports of miracles—God's supernatural intervention into people's lives that either defies laws of physics or, because of its timing and the odds against it, points directly to divine power. Some of these miracles I've believed, others I haven't. I've become more accepting of them lately, though, as I've witnessed a few myself. And because I've actually seen some now, I've sometimes found myself in the position of Mary Magdalene—my own eyewitness report rejected because it didn't fit the theology of the person I was telling it to. If people's faith and experience make them predisposed to reject a miracle, eyewitness reports usually aren't enough evidence for them.

Once when I told a Christian friend about a miracle I'd seen during a church service in another city, he responded, "I don't see how that would glorify God." It was a minor healing, and he saw it as having only cosmetic value, which, of course, God would never be interested in. (Apparently God's miracle-working power is so scarce that it needs to be rationed only to those who have the most serious needs.) He certainly believed in the possibility of miracles because they're in the Bible, and he even believed that miracles happened today. But for some reason, he was convinced I'd been fooled.

"Okay," I answered, "but I saw it."

"Maybe the lady was faking it."

"Well, her tears were very real and her emotions were very genuine. Either that, or she's better than most Academy Award nominees."

"You can't know if someone's genuine just by being with them for a couple of days."

"But you weren't there even for a couple of minutes. Since I was with her for a couple of days, isn't my account more reliable than your opinion that someone you've never met is lying?"

"Maybe, but I don't believe God would do something that frivolous."

"Hey, I was as skeptical as you are, so I was very careful to check it out."

"You probably couldn't get a close enough look."

"I was sitting right next to her for several hours that day."

"You weren't watching her the whole time, were you?"

"No, but I saw her get healed."

"You *think* you saw her get healed."

It's hard to express how frustrating this exchange was. If I'd told my friend that a ministry colleague was spreading an absurd rumor about him—not a likely occurrence considering the strong Christian character of our mutual colleagues—he'd have believed me without question. But all of a sudden I was unreliable because I reported something that didn't fit his expectations, something that didn't compare to anything he'd ever seen with his own eyes. Therefore, I, his once-trusted and respected friend, was suddenly a gullible fool.

This kind of skepticism has been true throughout Christian history, even from the earliest days. The apostles encountered many rejections for their claim that Jesus had been raised from death.[2] Paul once declared that he was on trial for the resurrection of the dead.[3] The Pharisees did a lot of fact-checking to disprove some of Jesus' miracles (in particular, the healing of the blind man as recorded in John 9:18), but they could never do so. In each case, suspicion was considered wise by human standards— "discerning," we like to call it to sound scriptural and spiritual—but disobedient by God's standards.

Most of us don't like anyone to make a fool of us, so we regard everything with suspicion. But nowhere in the Bible are we cautioned against looking foolish for having too much faith. In fact, we're told that the foolishness of God is wiser than the wisdom of men.[4] Paul said that he and the other apostles had become a spectacle to both men and angels. "We are fools for Christ's sake," he wrote in 1 Corinthians 4:10. Having already

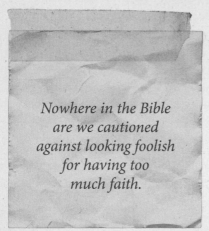

*Nowhere in the Bible are we cautioned against looking foolish for having too much faith.*

abandoned all attachment to our own reputation, we're free to believe God for the impossible (and even for the somewhat ridiculous). And if we fall on our face every once in a while, that's okay. God won't laugh at us for being too trusting. He'll honor simple faith more often than we think.

Where did we get off track? Skepticism has been around ever since Eden, but it became the official doctrine of whole societies during the Enlightenment. That's when we decided that the five senses were the only reliable means of determining what's true. The scientific method rules out supernaturalism as the product of primitive imaginations and superstitious simpletons. This is the lens through which academia has researched not only the "hard sciences" like physics and biology but also the social sciences like sociology and psychology. And this approach filters over into our explanations of history as well. Anything that can be explained in naturalistic terms is explained that way by default. And anything that can't be explained in those terms is assumed to have such an explanation even though we haven't figured it out just yet. The modern mind has been saturated in empirical processes and rationalistic expectations.

As evangelicals, we have our own variation on this theme. We've been steeped in modernism, the effects of which will linger long into the postmodern era, so we tend to explain our own experiences in naturalistic terms. But we also believe the Bible, so we explain the miracles of long ago as exactly that: miracles. The result is a theoretical supernaturalism that has no real relevance to our everyday lives. We may believe in miracles if they're far enough removed from our own experiences. (Have you ever noticed, for example, how Christians are much more likely to believe reports of miracles from other countries than those from our own neighborhoods?) But we certainly don't expect to see one. And if we do happen to see one, our knee-jerk reaction is to come up with a reason that it happened.

That's why, when we hear of a miracle we didn't see with our own eyes, our first response is to doubt the logic of the one telling us—even when the one telling us is someone we've trusted for years. "Did you see that yourself?" we ask. "How do you know it was real?" And our minds go racing for explanations.

Do you realize what kind of statement that makes to the people around us, to angelic observers, and even to our own hearts? It says that it's easier for us to doubt the credibility of people we know, love, and respect than it is for us to believe God would exercise his power to intervene in his own creation. It says that we have more faith that God won't do a miracle than that he will.

Those implicit statements may seem subtle, but they have profound consequences. For one thing, the more we reinforce that perspective, the harder it becomes for us to pray for God's intervention in our lives with any measure of real faith. Our hearts harden, and faith finds no footing there. That's tragic, considering that the Bible we profess to believe says it's impossible to please God without faith.[5] Jesus made it clear that miracles come through faith. *If* we have faith the size of a mustard seed, we can move mountains.[6] He will do for us *according to* our faith.[7] And, in one of the most surprising incidents in the New Testament, Jesus did do few miracles in his hometown because of their lack of faith.[8] Clearly, God responds supernaturally to our faith. We certainly can't say in the absence of a miracle that the believer didn't believe enough; that's only one possibility among many for an unanswered prayer. But while missing a miracle doesn't necessarily imply weak faith, weak faith almost always means missing a miracle.

It should be obvious that the Christian faith depends on believing the testimony of others. It's true that everyone needs to have a personal

> *While missing a miracle doesn't necessarily imply weak faith, weak faith almost always means missing a miracle.*

relationship with the Lord, but it's also true that getting into a relationship with him involves believing what others have said about him. When we believe any part of what the Bible says, we're believing the testimony of someone we never met. John's first letter even spells this out up front.

He tells his readers that he proclaims "what we have heard, what we have seen with our eyes, what we have looked at and touched with our hands, concerning the Word of Life . . . what we have seen and heard we proclaim to you also" (1 John 1:1, 3). In other words, "You didn't see these miracles, but we did, and we're trustworthy. Believe our reports."

That doesn't mean that we should accept everything we hear without any discernment. It simply means that our first response should be to assume that the miracle in question is a real possibility and, if the report comes from someone we trust, more of a probability. Instead of assuming a counterfeit and having to be convinced that it's real, assume it's real until you are convinced that it's counterfeit. There's nothing wrong with childlike faith. In fact, it's commanded.

C. S. Lewis made this point in an amusing way in *The Lion, the Witch and the Wardrobe*. After both Lucy and Edmund, the two youngest Pevensie children, had accidentally visited the strange land of Narnia, Lucy was adamant that the experience was real. Out of spite, Edmund said they had only been pretending. Their older brother and sister, Peter and Susan, discussed Lucy's "delusion" with the professor in whose home they were staying. The professor asked them:

> "Does your experience lead you to regard your brother or your sister as the more reliable? I mean, which is the more truthful?"
>
> "That's just the funny thing about it, sir," said Peter. "Up till now, I'd have said Lucy every time."
>
> "And what do you think, my dear?" said the Professor, turning to Susan.
>
> "Well," said Susan, "in general, I'd say the same as Peter, but this couldn't be true—all this about the wood and the Faun."
>
> "That is more than I know," said the Professor, "and a charge of lying against someone you have always found truthful is a very serious thing; a very serious thing indeed."
>
> "We were afraid it mightn't even been lying," said Susan; "we thought there might be something wrong with Lucy."
>
> "Madness, you mean?" said the Professor quite coolly. "Oh, you can make your minds easy about that. One has only to look at her and talk to her to see that she is not mad."

"But then," said Susan, and stopped. She had never dreamed that a grown-up would talk like the Professor and didn't know what to think.

"Logic!" said the Professor half to himself. "Why don't they teach logic at these schools? There are only three possibilities. Either your sister is telling lies, or she is mad, or she is telling the truth. You know she doesn't tell lies and it is obvious that she is not mad. For the moment then and unless any further evidence turns up, we must assume she is telling the truth."[9]

Primarily from anecdotal evidence, I believe both genuine miracles and their counterfeits are increasing in our days, and we should have higher priorities than trying to weed out the false from the true. God never told us to test the miracles; we're supposed to test the spirits behind them.[10] Are they done in the name of Jesus? Does the driving force of a miracle result in Jesus being praised? Do the people involved carry themselves with humility and selflessness? Do the miracles happen in a context of Christ-centered worship? Is the Cross—the sacrificial death and resurrection of Jesus on our behalf—a prominent theme in the environment in which these miracles take place?[11] Unless the answer to any of these questions is an emphatic and obvious no, I think we have to *want* not to believe a miracle to actually disbelieve it. There's no support in Scripture for viewing supernatural events with suspicion. We'll need to sense the truth of the teaching that accompanies those miracles, but we don't have to apply naturalistic standards to them. Let's just go ahead and accept them as "probably true"—after all, God's supernatural intervention should be commonplace enough not to surprise us—and then ask questions later if the major doctrinal beliefs of the people involved seem questionable. There's nothing sinful about believing a miracle that turns out to be false. But according to Jesus' rebuke of his disciples, there's something very sinful about disbelieving a miracle that turns out to be true.

Besides, it only makes sense that if we are being conformed to the image of Jesus—the same Jesus who healed and fed thousands and rose from the dead—that we'll be open to supernatural intervention. And if we're reluctant to believe that God can and will demonstrate his power through us and around us, then we're denying the fact that he has a pretty good track record doing exactly that. We're looking at his own testimony about himself and calling his past works unusual and unlikely to happen again, at least in our lives. And that's a far cry from biblical discipleship.

## FORGOTTEN MESSAGES FROM THE DISCIPLES:

+ You don't have to see a miracle to believe it happened.
+ Jesus always preferred childlike acceptance over sophisticated skepticism.
+ Rationalism has its limits. It can even be dangerous when it blinds us to God's greater possibilities.
+ The work of God and the word *explainable* really have very little to do with each other. That's a hard pill to swallow in a post-Enlightenment world, but it's true.

# CHAPTER 4

# FALLEN BUT NOT FORGOTTEN

Louis, chairman of the board of directors for Whole Peace Ministries, and Kevin, the ministry's chief financial officer, survey the ministry's warehouse. It's eerily quiet, and a sad emptiness seems to linger in the air. No one's working late tonight; it's a time for grief.

"Kevin, what do you think we should do with all of our inventory?"

"I don't know. Write it off and donate it to a mission field, maybe?"

"What mission field would take it?"

"Somewhere where they have no idea who he is."

"I don't think you realize how well known our president is, Kevin."

"Surely there's someplace in the world that didn't get the news about his . . . um, indiscretions."

"Maybe so, but even if they don't know now, I'd hate for them to read his books and watch his videos and then find out he's gone off the deep end."

"You don't think people will be willing to forgive him, Lou? You know what a short memory the public has."

"About brief immorality, yes. About immorality plus heretical statements on a nationally aired talk show, no. Not a chance. Anyway, we're not talking about the general public. They'll elect a guy to office or pay to see a movie star no matter what he's done. We're talking about Christians. Evangelicals. With our audience, once a man has fallen this far, he's always down."

"You're probably right, but I still think there may be a way. Give it time, some tears of repentance, and a completely new image, and perhaps they'll start buying his books again."

"New books, sure. Not these. The 'my story' books he writes later may sell millions just for their sordid details, but in the meantime, we've got operating expenses and a storeroom full of books and videos no one will ever buy. I think we're done, Kevin."

"Yeah, I know. I guess I was mainly just answering your question about inventory, not the viability of the ministry. I've already talked with our attorneys about setting up a meeting to go over bankruptcy procedures."

"I should probably break it to our staff pretty soon."

"I'm sure they already know it's only a matter of time. I suspect half of them have sent their résumés out already."

"Well, the sooner we make it official, the better for them."

"Lou, how do you think he got to this point? I mean, he went to a good seminary, was well grounded, founded this ministry, and has seen the fruit of it for more than two decades. He's seen God working here. How could he just throw that all away?"

"I don't know, Kevin. I can understand how somebody gives in to sexual temptation in a weak moment. It's probably even harder for a high-profile minister to resist. Satan would do anything to stop what God's been doing here. But dabbling in New Age practices after being so clear about the gospel for all those years? That's not a slipup in the heat of the moment. I don't get that at all."

"Yeah, me either. I bet his critics are laughing their heads off. Christians can be brutal."

"Have you heard any of the backlash yet?"

"You mean other than the 80 percent drop-off in sales?"

"Yeah. The magazine articles and Web sites and radio shows. As far as they're concerned, all of this proves what they've suspected all along. You know how it is; when a minister falls, everything he ever taught is suddenly false teaching—or might as well be."

"That's what I don't understand, Lou. The reverend had an effective ministry that changed a lot of people's lives. Listeners and readers wrote in by the boatloads telling him how God had used his words at just the right moment to do something dramatic in their lives. And now it's like, 'Oh, he sinned and now he's teaching heresy. He's a deceiver. Everything he ever said must be a lie.'"

"Yeah, I know. It's like we have some kind of illusion that real truth comes from somebody who's just as infallible as the Word or just as holy as the Holy Spirit. And then when the teacher shows how human he is, all of his words are under suspicion. I wouldn't be surprised if people start talking about how they knew deep down all along that he was under the influence of demonic powers and was really never saved to begin with."

"You're probably right. And we're lumped in with that too, you know. Everything *we've* ever believed is suspect too. We'll be considered fools for working with a man all those 'discerning' Christians just *knew* was false—even though most of them never said anything until now. He had a pretty big bandwagon, but no one will claim to have ever been on it."

"I can hear it now: 'See, this is what his kind of beliefs lead to! This just goes to show you how empty that kind of life is. He told people what they wanted to hear, not what they needed to hear. He's a hypocrite!' "

"Well, I still think he was a great Bible teacher and had a real pastor's heart. Probably still does. He just felt the pressure and blew it. That doesn't invalidate his whole ministry before now."

"Yeah. A sinner who becomes a preacher is a celebrity at church, but a preacher who becomes a sinner? The vultures swarm. As far as the public's concerned, his whole ministry—and the ministry we've devoted ourselves to for years—must have always been a sham."

+ + + +

It's tragic when a high-profile minister falls to temptation, has an emotional breakdown, or lets his doctrine deviate from the truth. It's disillusioning to the people who were fed by his ministry, and it becomes ammunition for those who were critical of it. Teaching once considered profound and life-changing is suddenly seen as empty and impotent, or maybe even blatantly deceptive. If the minister had a TV program, it's taken off the air. If he had published any books, they drop off the bestseller lists and into bargain bins immediately. And if he had a congregation, his church starts looking for a new pastor. Any way you look at it, a fallen leader fractures the body of Christ.

That's why it's absolutely fascinating that we read the works of Solomon as inspired Scripture. It *is* inspired Scripture, of course, and it's right for us to read and study the wisdom of Proverbs, the beauty of the Song of Solomon, and even the perspective of Ecclesiastes. What's strange is not that we appreciate Solomon's teachings, it's that we don't give the same grace to anyone today who does far less scandalous things than Solomon ever did. If Solomon had been teaching and writing today and then faltered as he did, Proverbs would be thrown into the evangelical Dumpster.

Don't believe me? Then pick any modern-day high-profile minister, politician, or business leader. (Let's stick with men in order to get the full force of Solomon's situation.) Got his name and face in your mind? Now imagine a front-page story reporting on the hundreds of women who have recently come out and admitted that they have slept with him over the years.[1] All of these women tell similar stories of the unimaginable luxury of his home—especially his bedroom. Imagine also a recent revelation that this minister was clinically depressed and getting treatment for several emotional disorders. As the story unfolds, it turns out that he has "networked" in all of the countries he's traveled to by arranging sexual unions between himself and the daughters of dignitaries. And, in his dalliances, he's been seen to worship at the shrines and temples of these young ladies' various religions. Then it all starts to make sense: *No wonder he's so empty and depressed,* you think. *He's not living close to God like he used to. He's filling his life with money and sex and even false worship. He has fallen away.*

> *If Solomon had been teaching and writing today and then faltered as he did, Proverbs would be thrown into the evangelical Dumpster.*

How many of this man's books—one of them a collection of erotic poems that you once thought to be only symbolic—will you go back and read for your own edification? How many sermons or speeches do you think he'll be invited to deliver now? How many of his leadership practices and life philosophies will you implement in your own life and work? The answers should be obvious. Yet in Solomon's case, we read his words of wisdom like they're the breath of life. And they are.

That's because Solomon started out well. The son of David and Bathsheba, Solomon was given an amazing offer by God himself: "Ask for whatever you want me to give you" (2 Chronicles 1:7, NIV). Solomon asked for wisdom and knowledge instead of wealth, victory, and long life, and because he answered so nobly, God gave him all of the above. He became the king who built the first Temple of Jerusalem, and God blessed the effort with his overwhelming presence and glory. During Solomon's reign, Israel's territory expanded farther than it ever had or ever would again. People came from far and wide to hear his wisdom, to see his building projects, and to marvel at his splendor. He had peace on every side.[2]

But Solomon certainly didn't finish well. Here's the rest of the story, according to the Bible:

> Now King Solomon loved many foreign women along with the daughter of Pharaoh: Moabite, Ammonite, Edomite, Sidonian, and Hittite women, from the nations concerning which the LORD had said to the sons of Israel, "You shall not associate with them, nor shall they associate with you, for they will surely turn your heart away after their gods." Solomon held fast to these in love. He had seven hundred wives, princesses, and three hundred concubines, and his wives turned his heart away. For when Solomon was old, his wives turned his heart away after other gods; and his heart was not wholly devoted to the LORD his God, as the heart of David his father had been. For Solomon went after Ashtoreth the goddess of the Sidonians and after Milcom the detestable idol of the Ammonites. Solomon did what was evil in the sight of the LORD, and did not follow the LORD fully, as David his father had done. Then Solomon built a high place [i.e., altar] for Chemosh the detestable idol of Moab, on the mountain which is east of Jerusalem, and for Molech the detestable idol of the sons of Ammon. Thus also he did for all his foreign wives, who burned incense and sacrificed to their gods. (1 KINGS 11:1-8)

Obviously, God wasn't pleased with this sort of behavior, and he vowed to tear the kingdom out of Solomon's hand, or rather out of the hand of Solomon's son—a promise he fulfilled decisively. What the Bible then shows us, much of it from Solomon's own hand in Ecclesiastes, is a sad picture of disillusionment, angst, and despair. Solomon grew frustrated with life and seems to have faded away into depression and eventually death. In spite of all of his early blessings, he was not a happy man.

This leaves us with an interesting dilemma, doesn't it? Solomon did things that provoked God to anger, and God judged him for those things.

But the words God had given Solomon before his apostasy remain inspired. Some of the words Solomon wrote after his apostasy remain inspired too.[3] So we have a choice: Do we read the words of a philandering, idol-worshiping zillionaire as inspired truth that teaches us of God's wisdom? Or do we reject the works of someone whose later life was filled with blatant disobedience and severe chastisement from God?

The answer, of course, is that if the philandering, idol-worshiping zillionaire is named Solomon and part of inspired Scripture, we preach about his words and have small-group studies to learn them more thoroughly. And if the philandering, idol-worshiping zillionaire is not named Solomon, we relegate him to the trash heap and never think of him again, except in derision.

The real question behind that choice is this: When God works through someone, does that work remain valid, regardless of the course that person takes in the future? The scriptural answer is yes; God does valid work through people who will fall. The modern-day Christian answer is no; if a person doesn't finish well, it means he must never have been well to begin with.

*God does valid work through people who will fall.*

We have this same dilemma with David, too, you know. If I committed adultery and arranged for the "accidental" death of a friend, this book would be in your next garage sale (and you'd probably need to pay someone to take it). And I don't imagine you'd ever see one of my books on a store shelf again. But those twin sins are exactly what David did, and we read the psalms he wrote—before, during, and after this episode of his life—as some of our favorite portions of Scripture. No one, as far as I know, has ever read the Twenty-third Psalm and said, "Gee, what a hypocrite that David was. How'd we ever fall for that syrupy 'praise the Lord' act? Looks like the shepherd boy was really a wolf after all!" No, we read that psalm and many others as some of the clearest expressions of the heart of God—and of a man who sought that heart passionately.

How would we counsel people who fell like this today? We might not even try—after all, they know more answers than we do. We might simply ask them the obvious questions: "How could you have so much and throw it all away? How could you know the truth so well and then disobey it? How could you fellowship with the Lord and bear so much fruit and then turn away?" But even they wouldn't be able to answer such questions.

The lessons we learn from David, Solomon, and other fallen heroes of Scripture are many. For one thing, we learn that God can use anyone and, in fact, often prefers to work through people who are weak and flawed. This highlights his mercy, which is more than enough to bring redemption out of the deepest kinds of depravity; his power, which doesn't depend on human strength for anything; and his wisdom, which is displayed better among fools than among know-it-alls. We also learn that not everyone who falls away had an evil heart to begin with. And we learn furthermore that a tragic, sinful collapse does not hinder God from working through someone again. God worked through both Solomon and David after their worst deeds, and he continues to work through the worship and wisdom they wrote down. They still impact our lives for God's glory today.

But one of the saddest lessons we learn from Solomon and David is that God's heart toward leaders who have fallen is opposed by most Christians. In other words, modern evangelicalism in general disagrees with God about the contributions that influential but sinful Christians can make. He and we do not have the same heart.

That's a huge accusation, but it's true. Certainly there are individual exceptions—the church today includes plenty of gracious people—but the loudest voices when a leader falls are scathing, blistering attacks on the person's integrity, doctrine, works, followers, methodology, and fruitfulness. And certainly it's appropriate to insist on a time of restoration rather than putting a leader right back into his or her responsibilities. But our general perspective seems harsher, that one public sin is big enough to invalidate a lifetime of faithfulness. And we frequently take to the airwaves to say so.

That's not God's perspective. God is in the business of overcoming ugly blots of sin that stain a person's life. In God's eyes, no one leading any church or ministry today is perfect. Behind the scenes, everyone has stains. That's not a problem for God; the message of the gospel is that stains are removed by the blood of Jesus. But those who are most vocal about the blood of Jesus are often those most unwilling to apply it to a Christian who sins. And that's a worse hypocrisy than the kind they accuse a fallen leader of committing.

We've had plenty of opportunities in the last couple of decades to witness the fall of high-profile ministers, and it's a painful picture to watch. The church gets ridiculed by outsiders and insiders alike, the people who trusted the ministers are disillusioned, and every truth ever taught by those ministers is called into question. These reactions are understandable—to a point. But why are they so permanent and so sweeping?

My aim isn't to defend every fallen minister out there. Some of them really were false teachers who never functioned in the flow of God's Spirit. Vicious wolves among the flock are a reality, and some of them have lied and pretended for years in order to deceive people and make a buck. I even know of a few who have been willing tools of the enemy. But that's certainly not true of all of them. Some of them are godly people who subtly and gradually developed patterns of weakness that were exploited at opportune moments by spiritual enemies of the gospel. That's the same dynamic, by the way, that occurs in your life and mine. Only in ours, it's not on camera. No one will write about our frailties in magazines or discuss them on talk shows. No, our falls are reasonably obscure. We may experience some upturned noses and not-so-subtle whispers, but most of us don't make headlines. But public falls are very, very messy.

Let me make it clear that I'm not in any way recommending turning a blind eye to serious sin. The church should be zealous about its purity. God was certainly zealous about Solomon's and David's purity, and he made that clear in the way he dealt with them for their sins. But God didn't spew out venomous personal attacks, and he didn't declare the entire ministry of these two kings null and void. When there are offenses in the church, the Christian community should deal with those offenses, not cannibalize the offender. False teaching should be pointed out, discipline should be imposed for immorality and financial mismanagement, and remedies should be sought out for addictions and ongoing emotional or relational issues. And wolves should be swiftly and completely removed from the flocks. But sweeping statements of judgment against people who have had genuine ministries? That hardly seems biblical. It's one thing to deal compassionately and redemptively with a fallen leader. That can be done decisively and even sternly while maintaining an attitude of humility. But it's quite another thing for those outside of the situation to rise up in outrage and publicly castigate prominent Christians. That's one way to ensure that the world will *not* know us for our love.

If you think this is simply a matter of how you react when Rev. So-and-So gets caught in a compromising situation, look a little closer. There are implications for how all of us live as Christians. Human beings generally follow the model presented to them by their leadership. That applies to the church just as much as any other social group—more so, actually.[4] So when our leaders—who have observed those who have fallen before them and realize what it would mean if they show any hint of vulnerability or admit to any struggles—feel pressured to act like they have it all together, we follow their lead. The result is an entire culture of Christians who are afraid to take their masks off. This cultivates a general perception in the church that to be a good Christian means having it all together.

> *When there are offenses in the church, the Christian community should deal with those offenses, not cannibalize the offender.*

That has changed quite a bit in the last couple of decades, but the tendency is still there, especially among those in large ministries and high-profile roles. It's easy to see why; we've seen what happens when vocal critics witness a downfall—or even a minor slipup, for that matter. They blackball ministers for being human.

The truth is that the church today wouldn't tolerate leaders like Solomon and David. A lot of people would be on these rulers' bandwagons when all was well, of course, but after their egregious errors, most would deny that a bandwagon ever even existed. And Psalms and Proverbs would simply be historical relics, not inspired masterpieces. Our councils and committees would never have included them in any sacred compilation. They would be nothing more than the ramblings of two men who disgraced themselves in the midst of God's people.

**FORGOTTEN MESSAGES FROM SOLOMON:**
+ Sometimes we're supposed to do as someone says and not as he does.
+ The inspiration of the Holy Spirit in a person's life is not nullified by any later contradictions to it in that person's lifestyle or beliefs.
+ God sometimes chooses to use people he knows will one day fall flat on their faces and dishonor him.

# THAT SEEMS SINFUL

THERE WERE PLENTY OF REASONS the scribes and priests of Jesus' day rejected his teaching—his extravagant claims, his unexplainable miracles, his unconventional style, to name a few. But one of the primary reasons was that all of his works and teachings came in the context of what looked like sin. He *seemed* disobedient on quite a few points. He didn't always follow God's law about the Sabbath, for example, or about ritual cleanliness. He spent quite a bit of time with sinners and even favored them over the most upstanding members of society. He ignored a lot of rules.

Naturally, the religious leaders pointed this out. They said he cast out demons by the power of Satan. They said things like, "This man is not from God" (John 9:16) and, "We know that this man is a sinner" (John 9:24). And because of the lenses through which they viewed the Bible, they were completely blinded to the righteousness of the Son of God. He was the only human being ever to live a sinless life, and they called him a sinner.

Do we do the same thing with many of God's servants? It depends on the criteria we use, but I believe in many cases we do. What looks sinful to our righteous eyes is often the work of God. That may sound like an offensive charge, but the Pharisees were offended, too, and their offense was no indicator that they were right. When we bristle at the thought that we might be rejecting God's works because they look unrighteous to us, maybe that's a sign that we need to look a little closer. His ways aren't always palatable to religious minds.

+ + + +

# CHAPTER 5

# TREACHEROUS FAITH

Chicago, November 11—Prominent community leader Abe Terawicz was arrested this morning on charges of attempted murder after confessing that he tied up his son and raised a knife over his throat as though making a ritual sacrifice last Friday. Terawicz set the knife down at the last moment, leaving both him and his son shaken but unharmed.

Terawicz's son, Isaac—the only eyewitness to the crime—described the bizarre incident simply as an act of devotion and said he held no hard feelings against his father. Asked if he would file for a restraining order, the younger Terawicz said, "No, I don't think there's any need for that. God knows how to restrain him when necessary."

Terawicz's wife, Sarah, was seen briefly talking to police and was visibly distraught. She was unavailable for comment to the media.

If convicted, Terawicz could face considerable time in prison. However, the judge assigned to the case could choose to take into account the fact that he voluntarily stopped the attack and reduce the charge to threat with a deadly weapon. That would result in substantially less prison time than a typical sentence for attempted murder. Whether there will be any further charges stemming from the incident is unclear.

Reactions from neighbors and the larger community ranged from outrage to morbid fascination. Some were simply stunned. "He seemed so nice," said longtime neighbor Roger Michaels. "A little eccentric maybe, but never capable of something like this. Very well respected. I'm speechless."

Because of the incident, the FBI is launching an investigation into the form of Judaism practiced by the family, throwing a spotlight not only on the cultlike upbringing of Terawicz's children—it's probable but uncertain that he has more than one—but also on the Jewish community as a whole. But Rabbi Ezra Cohen was quick to distance mainstream Judaism from smaller sects like that of the Terawicz family.

"One thing that's clear from our Scripture is that God is opposed to child sacrifice," Cohen said. "The ancient tribes of Canaan used to burn their children or make blood sacrifices of them in their worship of idols, and Scripture always, *always* portrays this as an abomination to God. These were really gruesome practices, very brutal. This is simply a resurrection of a deviant theology, and our faith condemned this sort of thing long ago."

Leaders of the Christian community voiced similar objections, pointing out the violent nature of many of its spin-off sects and cults.

"Even though many children in the neighborhood loved him, this is obviously not the kind of man you want to be influencing your kids," said Jim Johnson, pastor of Fellowship Church, just two blocks from the Terawicz home. "This is such a blight on the community of faith and a terrible model for our young people."

Though Terawicz has no previous record of legal violations, his family life has been considered by friends and acquaintances to be somewhat unconventional and, in the words of some, "alarming." It was widely rumored years ago, for example, that he fathered a son through the family's housekeeper, who was subsequently forced out of the home to live on the street.

The alleged estranged son has not been in contact with the family for years but, if found, could possibly be called as a witness in Terawicz's upcoming trial, as could the former housekeeper. Both would provide insight into the secret world of the family's relational dynamics and religious practices.

A trial date will be set next week after a preliminary hearing.

+ + + +

Genesis 22 is one of the most heartrending passages of Scripture. The voice of God came to Abraham clearly enough for this father to take his beloved, long-awaited son up on a mountain and offer him as a sacrifice. There's no indication of Abraham's struggle to obey. Early the next morning, he and Isaac left with everything he needed to perform a ritual sacrifice. From Isaac's point of view, the only thing missing was the sacrifice itself.

It had to be a very awkward trip. Could Isaac tell how heavy his father's heart was? Or was this just another father-son outing? As for Abraham, his mind must have been as filled with questions as his heart was with dread. What would happen to God's promise of many descendants now, if the only son of promise was no longer around? Would it be fulfilled through Sarah again? Or through another wife in his even older age?[1] And what would he tell Sarah when he returned? "Honey, I'm sorry, but our Isaac won't be coming home. I know you longed for him for years and that you have loved him dearly ever since he was born, but he had to be sacrificed. God told me to." That would have been history's most strained marriage. Everything in Abraham's life would be turned upside down by this event. Things would never be the same.

The trip back home had to be pretty awkward too. Though Abraham's heart may have been lighter than air because he never had to go through with the offering, Isaac's heaviness may have just begun. Why would his own father raise a knife to kill him? Would Abraham ever again think God told him to do that? Would Isaac ever feel comfortable being alone with his father now? And how would his mother react to this strange trip? Or did she already know? Was she in on it too? Would he have to be careful around her as well? Was it perhaps time to leave home and move to a distant land?

Looking back on this episode in Abraham's life, all we see is the amazing faith he demonstrated and the fruit of his obedience. We assume that this sort of thing must have been more acceptable in a primitive culture and much less shocking. And perhaps it was—there were at least precedents of child sacrifice in the area and no police force patrolling the neighborhood—but it was still offensive and, from all outward appearances, evil. But none of that speculation resolves the dilemma for us. We can't just say it was different back then and move on with the spiritual lessons. This episode raises a problem for us that we normally don't attempt to resolve.

The problem is that this offensive, evil-looking assignment came straight out of the heart of God, regardless of the culture in which it took place. And since God's heart doesn't change, his willingness to allow his choice servants to appear offensive and irrational remains. It is entirely within his character to lead his people in directions that look absolutely wrong to us.

If a man walked into one of our churches and said God told him

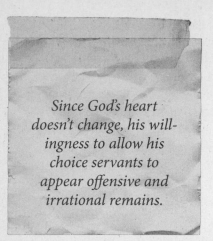

*Since God's heart doesn't change, his willingness to allow his choice servants to appear offensive and irrational remains.*

to sacrifice his son on an altar, we'd seek immediate help for him. We'd tell him that God doesn't contradict himself; he said, "Thou shalt not kill," and he would therefore not tell anyone today to kill. We'd remind him that child sacrifice was a pagan practice and that God calls it an abomination in his Word.[2] We'd talk to him about how to discern the voice of God from demonic voices. Many of us would conclude he was at least delusional and perhaps even filled with a spirit of evil. And if he were committed to a mental institution on the grounds of being a danger to himself and others, we wouldn't be surprised in the least.

But God sacrificed his own Son, and he's not filled with a spirit of evil. And he's the one who commanded Abraham to sacrifice his son. Yes, it's true that he didn't let Abraham go through with it, but that's not the point. Abraham was put in a position of having to believe that God *would* let him go through with it—that this *was* consistent with God's character. God wouldn't ask his servant to trust a false image of himself. He gave Abraham a true image and said, "Trust me and follow me."

I've heard of a new convert in North Africa who followed in Abraham's footsteps in obedience to God, but in his case, no angel stopped the knife and his son was killed. That's heartbreaking. Because Abraham's intended sacrifice pointed to God's sacrifice and resurrection of his beloved Son centuries later, any subsequent sacrifice of this nature seems unnecessary and anticlimactic. It's extremely unlikely that God would ask anyone today to pack a knife and take a little father-son trip to a mountain for that purpose. But the report of this new believer sacrificing his son did raise some of these questions in my mind. If I react so negatively to someone doing that today, wouldn't I have acted negatively against Abraham in his day? And because God had commanded Abraham to do this—without telling him ahead of time that an angel would prevent him from following through with the sacrifice—wouldn't I then have been opposing God's will? Was there any moment in the last four thousand years when God said, "I will no longer ask my servants to do such strange things"? I can't find one.

If you're feeling a little uncomfortable with God right now, that's good. He wants us to have an extremely intimate relationship with him, but our closeness doesn't imply predictability or even a complete sense of safety. It's true that his love casts out all fear,[3] but it doesn't cast out all discomfort. In Christ, we can know that we're safe from his punishment. But also in Christ, we're called to danger-ous adventures that involve challeng-ing the status quo, radically obeying his lead, calling on him to do great things in our midst, and risking our lives for the sake of his name. There's no prom-ise in Scripture that God will leave us in our comfort zone. We have no in-dication that he won't offend us by the things he does in the people around us. There's no biblical evidence that when God moves, we won't be shocked or even confused (see Acts 2 for an ex-ample). So when we're shocked, con-fused, offended, or uncomfortable, we

*It's true that God's love casts out all fear, but it doesn't cast out all discomfort.*

can't say, "Well, God wouldn't put us through that." Yes, he would. He has already proven that. And he probably will again.

Try to imagine how you would react to these situations today:

+ The wealthiest man in the city, who happens to be a great bene-factor to your church, says God told him to walk away from it all and live in the woods—even though it will mean the end of his very fruitful ministry of financial generosity.
+ The most talented and popular musician in worship music today says God told him to throw his guitar over a cliff and stop singing. He doesn't know what he'll do next. He's just obey-ing God.
+ A woman who deeply loves her family says she's called by God to walk away for a couple of years and start a ministry. She doesn't know what kind of ministry yet. She makes

arrangements for the family's welfare while she's away, but she insists that this is the Lord's will.[4]

+ Seven young men with extremely promising careers decide at the end of their very expensive education to work in third-world obscurity rather than succeed in the professional world. Most of their peers can only say, "What a waste."[5]

Obviously, these examples don't come close to the trauma of Abraham's act of obedience. We might be pretty confused about these people's decision-making processes, and their claims to have heard God's voice would be questioned by many. But these give us a small taste of the offering on Mount Moriah long ago. I don't think that offering, in its specifics, is repeatable—which is why the examples above don't attempt to stretch our limits further than they do.[6] But I do believe in the radical nature of obedience and the need to be open to *anything* God might say. Preemptive discernment should never be allowed to weed out the voice of God before it takes root in our hearts. And clearly it didn't with Abraham. The voice came through loud and clear, and as bizarre as it seemed, Abraham obeyed.

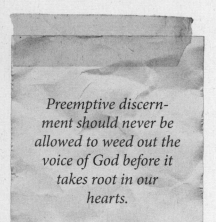

*Preemptive discernment should never be allowed to weed out the voice of God before it takes root in our hearts.*

What if God said something like that today? I don't mean the actual sacrifice of a child, obviously, because the ultimate sacrifice has already been given. (Plus, that's illegal and would get you twenty-to-life in a room without a view.) And I don't mean any other kind of behavior that clearly contradicts his character or violates his purposes.[7] Sometimes issues of obedience and disobedience really are obvious. But what if God fills his church with people who are asked to do radical acts of obedience that seem to defy logic and baffle observers? Will we join the chorus of critics and voice our "deep concerns" about embarrassing behavior and questionable doctrine? Or will we marvel at the ways of God, knowing that while some people have misheard his voice, many others are walking in the kind of faith through which God changes the course of history?

More important, what if God gave you a radical assignment of obedience? Would your concerns about how it would look to others and your fears about possible consequences keep you from obeying? Would some Christians' pervasive warnings against saying "God told me" inhibit you from saying so, even though you were absolutely convinced he had spoken? Would you be more fearful of offending your church or of offending your God? If so, remember this: any Bible hero's relationship with God would have stretched his or her own faith and raised the suspicions of those around him or her. It's a tension that can't be resolved except in retrospect.

I believe these are critical questions for our generation because God is filling his church with people who follow him in radical, baffling extremes. In fact, he has always done that in some measure, and that measure seems to have begun to increase rapidly in recent years. The sacrificial commitment that seemed so remarkable of missionaries in eighteenth- and nineteenth-century contexts is found among many college students today. Groups of Christian students, for example, have marched the Silk Road from Hong Kong to Jerusalem in order to share Christ in every country they pass through—including those in which sharing Christ is illegal and very dangerous. They seem to understand that about half of them will become martyrs along the way, but they do it anyway. I've met people who have endured unspeakable torture without denying Jesus, who have forsaken fortunes and future careers for the sake of the gospel, and who have dedicated themselves to around-the-clock prayer movements for the Kingdom of God to increase on earth. In some circles, older Christians may rightly lament the apostasy of the next generation. But in most places, those laments ignore the thousands of radical worshipers who would die for Jesus at a moment's notice. Globally, the rising generation of believers is more committed than ever. As God continues to pour out his Spirit on his people, his people will continue to grow in the kind of faith

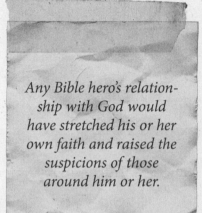

*Any Bible hero's relationship with God would have stretched his or her own faith and raised the suspicions of those around him or her.*

that defies all expectations. And while immense portions of the church will counsel against that sort of faith, calling it unbiblical, impractical, undignified, offensive, and even ungodly, those who love the Lord more than the opinions of others will not be moved.

## FORGOTTEN MESSAGES FROM ABRAHAM:

+ God isn't opposed to everything that looks wrong to us. He sometimes even *commands* things that look wrong to us.
+ God might ask us to sacrifice not only the things most precious to us, but also our reputations.
+ The meaning of symbolic acts may not be known until centuries later.

# CHAPTER 6
# A PROPHETIC HOOKUP

"Hey guys, I have an announcement. I'm getting married!"

"Whoa, you've been holding out on us. We had no idea you were even dating anyone! Isn't small group supposed to be a place where you can, like, *share* your life?"

"No offense, guys—I couldn't tell you about her until now. Actually, I haven't even known her that long, so there wasn't anything to tell . . . until recently."

"So? . . . Are you gonna tell us anything about her now?"

"Oh, yeah. Well, it's kind of a strange story. As you know, I've been praying about finding the right person, and a few weeks ago I started feeling led to, um . . . well, it's really weird. Are you sure you want to know?"

"Hey, we're your friends. Spill it."

"Okay, well, you know how we've been studying about how God speaks to people? I, um, heard him."

"Are you serious? That's awesome! What was it like?"

"It was so cool. It started out as a sudden thought, and so I asked him why I had that thought. And then it grew and grew until I was just about consumed with it. I mean, it really grew roots in me, and I couldn't get it out of my mind. So then I asked him what the deal was—why my heart just seemed to grab onto it, especially since it's pretty bizarre. I asked him for signs to confirm it too, and he gave me some—and, of course, some Bible verses that confirmed that this kind of thing is in his heart. So I followed. I obeyed. And, well, now I'm engaged."

"Um, you skipped the best part. Did he, like, point out a girl and say, 'That's her'? Or were you like, 'The next girl who walks through the doors of my dorm is the one'? How's that work?"

"No, it wasn't like that. I felt like he wanted me to go downtown and just find a girl on the street. I really think he wants me to make a point about how he loves us."

"So what do you mean? You just walked down the street and started talking to girls about whether they wanted to marry you? Like, 'If you're done shopping at that store, you wanna go commit to live with each other for the rest of our lives?'"

"Um, not exactly. I mean I didn't start with that. But I did walk up to one and say, 'I think God wants us to talk and maybe go out together.'"

"Wow, that's crazy!"

"Yeah, she thought so too. She laughed and told me that was the cheesiest line she'd ever heard. But, of course, she said she'd do . . . you know, whatever I wanted if she was 'worth it' to me."

"Wait, wait, wait. You mean, you accidentally went up to a hooker? Awww, man! That's hilarious!"

"Yeah. I mean, no, not accidentally. But yeah, she was a hooker."

"So this is all a joke? I thought you were serious. Man, you had us going. You've got a really strange sense of humor. Like you'd really ever have the nerve to talk to a hooker!"

"No, no. I'm not kidding. This isn't a joke. Turns out she didn't go for it, so I prayed, adjusted my approach, and the next girl started talking with me. We hung out for a couple of weeks—I mean, whenever she wasn't working and I wasn't in class—and then I proposed. She thinks I'm 'quirky' . . . and cute. So, mission accomplished. That's where God led me."

"C'mon. You don't expect us to believe that, do you?"

"Guys, I'm serious. I know it's weird. I'm not denying that. And I figured you guys would have a hard time accepting it. But really, I'm not kidding. God really did tell me to marry a prostitute."

"Did you miss the day we talked about how to tell if that voice is God's or not? This is a no-brainer. I hate to break it to you, but that isn't God. He wouldn't tell you to pick up a hooker and propose to her. That's insane."

"I know it sounds like that, but he even gave me an explanation. I saw it really clearly: he gave me a strong impression that our marriage was going to be a picture of how he feels about his people, even when they have an ugly past and aren't faithful to him."

"Okay, let's play along for a minute. There are so many things wrong with this that I don't even know where to begin. Look, you can't throw your life away like this. God has a really sweet, godly girl for you somewhere. You can't just 'hook up' with some streetwalker because you think you got an impression that maybe you should make a lifelong commitment to someone who's probably got forty kinds of herpes and worse. *And* someone you just met! What are you thinking? That she's gonna turn into a nice little housewife and take care of your babies while you're at work?"

"No, I doubt it. In fact, she'll probably cheat on me several times."

"Okay, good, now you're being realistic. So call her up and break it off, and then we'll pray really hard for God to bring the right girl into your life."

"No, I can't. God told me to do this. I know she'll probably sleep with other men even after we're married, but I'm supposed to be faithful to her anyway. I think it's supposed to be a picture of how God loves us even though we're unfaithful. That's the message God wants his churches to understand."

"Oh, my goodness. We're going to be praying for you anyway, 'cause this is just sick. Have you told your mom yet?"

"No, not yet. She'll freak. Worse than you guys."

"Yeah, you better believe worse than us. This will kill her, you know? And your dad will probably kill you."

"I know. I thought of that."

"Wow, I thought I'd done a pretty good job of leading this group. Not now . . . this isn't anything close to what we learned. Where'd we go wrong?"

"We didn't—you've done a great job. This is right. I'm convinced that this is what God said, and nothing's gonna change my mind about that."

"Man, there's no way you're going through with this. It's just freaky. You've *got* to come to your senses."

"You know, I figured you wouldn't understand—in fact, I'd be shocked if you did—but I thought at least that you'd be supportive."

"Supportive! Hey, we care about you. We can't be supportive of something this abnormal. The supportive thing is to confront you on it. I'm serious, you'll ruin your life. She'll give you diseases, break your heart, ruin you financially, abandon your kids—if you can stick it out long enough to have kids, that is—and bring all kinds of disgusting men into your life that you'll wish you'd never met. You'll wake up one day and realize you could've had a completely different life."

"I won't have any regrets if I know I'm following God."

"Listen, if you think she's good-looking and want to marry her because you can't wait for a wife any longer, go ahead. But don't pin it on God. I mean, if you have to marry a prostitute, then at least be man enough to claim responsibility for the decision. But you'll find out soon enough: if you don't do things God's way, you've got a *very* rough road ahead of you. A very rough road."

"Guys, I *am* doing things God's way."

"I honestly can't imagine God wishing this on anyone. Man, you're giving me a headache. So . . . are you going to introduce us to her sometime so we can at least see who's cast a spell on you?"

"Yeah, of course. I was hoping maybe on Monday night. She's working this weekend."

"Oh, man, that's gross. That's just nasty. You've absolutely lost your mind."

"So, Monday then?"

"Yeah, whatever."

✦ ✦ ✦ ✦

God told Hosea to marry an adulterous woman. We don't know for sure if Gomer was immoral before their marriage or committed adultery afterward, but we do know that God's original word to him was clear about what he was in for. He didn't find out later about her unfaithfulness; he knew it up front. He was to marry someone of shameful character who would cheat on him frequently. And she would bear children that he could only hope were actually his.

That doesn't sound much like God, does it? In fact, if someone came along claiming that sort of direction from God, we'd laugh. It would look like a poor excuse to endorse a sinful lifestyle. We'd probably see Hosea as a self-deluded lecher rationalizing his desire to marry a woman he had no business marrying. To our secular culture, his choice of a mate would look ridiculously foolish; to our churches, it would look shameful and sinful; and in his own culture, it was even more shockingly "ungodly." No matter how much Scripture he quoted to us and no matter how zealous he was about following God, if he knowingly married a prostitute,[1] we'd doubt his godliness—maybe even his salvation.

Why? Because God wouldn't tell someone to be yoked to an unbeliever, would he? That's unscriptural. So is the idea of marrying a woman who, according to the law God himself gave through Moses, should have been stoned after her first offense. If Hosea pastored a church today, the entire evangelical community would be publicly calling for his resignation. It would be an open scandal and entertaining fodder for sleazy tabloids. "Minister marries whore—and says God told him to!" He would be the butt of jokes and the target of discerning voices everywhere. We could find verse after verse proving that this kind of thing is *never* the will of God. Except it was.

Now, is this kind of thing normally God's will? Or even his will for more than this one Old Testament prophet? I seriously doubt it. The right to marry a prostitute is certainly not the purpose of this portion of Scripture, and it's definitely not a "right" worth defending. I can't even imagine a guy being willing to obey the Lord on this assignment. (I can't imagine a guy being willing to marry someone named Gomer either, but that's just me.) I also don't think it's wise to marry an unbeliever or to compromise with immorality. The calling to do either is exceptional; either action is almost always wrong. The point is not that Hosea's behavior should be emulated, but that his marriage is a prime example of something we'd assume is a violation of God's character. And yet God's character is what put him up to it.

That's because Hosea's life was meant to be a graphic picture of God's relationship with his people. To the surprise of many in Hosea's day and ours, God didn't mind portraying himself as a brokenhearted husband. He's majestic and unchanging for sure, but he's also, according to his own imagery, a jilted lover in the throes of grief. So he inspires Hosea to use some pretty explicit language, as in Hosea 2:14-23, for example, where he says he will allure Israel, betroth her, and inseminate her.[2] The prophet freely writes in vivid expressions designed to jolt the reader into a sudden awareness of the nation's sins. But the words of the prophet are still less offensive than his marriage, which must have looked completely unbecoming for a man of God. Yet this was God's plan for him.

Think about the observers in Hosea's day. Would they be any more tolerant of his actions than we would be? Would they say, "It's okay, he's a prophet—God must have told him to do this to illustrate a point"? No, they'd point fingers and call him a heretic for suggesting that God might have anything to do with his disgracefully lustful pursuits. Just like we would.

That point becomes self-evident when we personalize Hosea's story. For example, envision a man in your family or in your close circle of friends. Got a clear picture of his face in your mind? Good. Now imagine how you'd respond if he came to you and said that God sent him on a divine mission to marry a hooker. Would you keep an open mind? Or would you try to convince him that whatever voice he heard, it wasn't God's?

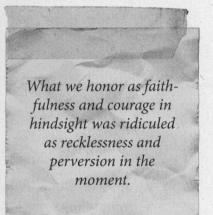

*What we honor as faithfulness and courage in hindsight was ridiculed as recklessness and perversion in the moment.*

Like nearly all prophets, Hosea is considered a great man of God—in retrospect. At the time, however, most people would have considered him a lunatic. What we honor as faithfulness and courage in hindsight is ridiculed as recklessness and perversion in the moment. That's because people who aren't sensitive to the movements of God—and even many who are—can't tell what's from God and what isn't until all the results are in. Unfortunately, that usually comes after those involved have been laughed at, persecuted, and in many cases, dead and buried for at least a few decades.

So how should this apply to our current perspective? Consider these examples:

+ A Christian college student claims that God leads him into bars every Friday and Saturday night to witness to people who are trying to forget how empty their life is.
+ A young missionary believes she's called to build relationships with girls in the red-light district by helping them fix their hair and do their makeup before a night's work—all so she can eventually teach them new skills and lead them to Christ.
+ A minister does not fight his daughter's decision to marry an

abusive drug addict so he can illustrate how God sometimes turns us over to our own self-destructive pursuits in the hope that one day we'll realize our error and return to him.

Are these acts of obedience or reckless disregard for God's will? The correct answer, of course, is that we don't know—not from this little bit of information, anyway. A lot of other variables are involved. What's the motive of each of these people? Did they really sense God's leading or were they just fooling themselves? Did the college student have addictive tendencies, and was he putting himself in a tempting situation? Or was he reasonably safe from the lure of alcohol? Was the young missionary woefully naive or divinely courageous? Did the minister have a passive approach to relationships that caused him to cop out with flimsy excuses about his daughter? Or did he really allow God to lead him to make such a hard sacrifice for God's purposes? No observer has enough information to make such judgments. These matters aren't for the methodology police to speculate about from the sidelines. They're between the called and the Caller.

The point isn't that these acts are inherently godly. They may or may not be, depending on variables like those mentioned. It's obviously wise to be extremely cautious about such things. The bottom line is that we can't say about any of them, "This is wrong because it violates God's character," or "Scripture forbids us from these acts because we're supposed to give no appearance of evil." The life of Hosea forces us to conclude that God might actually lead someone to do questionable things. Each of the examples I've given above pales in comparison to the scandal of Hosea's situation, and yet each has drawn harsh criticism from present-day Christians. If God could lead a great prophet into a marriage that appears to flaunt its shamefulness, then he really might lead someone today to do something that nearly all godly people would question—or even condemn. If the God of

*The life of Hosea forces us to conclude that God might actually lead someone to do questionable things.*

Hosea is the same God we worship, and if he doesn't change his personality every eon or so, then following him might be really embarrassing sometimes.

But we don't give people the room to follow God that way, do we? Many in the evangelical community are just as quick to throw stones as Paul was before he met Christ. If something hints of impropriety, we attack it.

Each of the examples above is based on a real-life situation. The third is exaggerated a little—I've only heard a minister make this kind of claim after the fact—but the other two are actual scenarios. In all three cases, well-meaning Christians who didn't know the particular people involved or all the details of the situation felt perfectly comfortable expressing their contempt for such flawed motives and/or methods. "God wouldn't do that," they said. Yet God has borne genuine fruit in these cases.

The "God wouldn't do that" rebuttal is a dead giveaway that someone is depending on theory rather than experience. (I know because I've said it plenty of times.) That statement uses the language of speculation, which means the person saying it doesn't really know what God *is* doing at the moment. It's hypothetical. When we have to use terms like *would* or *wouldn't* with another person, we're admitting that we don't actually have the facts from that person directly. We're guessing. Likewise, when we use those terms with God, we're acknowledging that he hasn't actually informed us of his opinion and that we don't really expect to hear his voice. In fact, it's a clear indication that we're not even going to ask him. We just know. He "wouldn't" do that.

That knee-jerk reaction reveals that the speaker hasn't read about—or has somehow forgotten—people like Hosea. If God would lead a righteous prophet in such an odd way, he could certainly lead people down strange paths today. And the only way to know if that's what God's doing is to be in a vibrant relationship with him and ask. Piecing together a patchwork standard from Scripture won't suffice; the structures we come up with when we try to reduce his Word to a formula can't contain God. We have to actually ask him to speak to us and listen as if we expect him to. If he chooses to reveal his will about someone else's calling, then he'll find a way to communicate his message to us. And if he doesn't . . . well, it really wasn't any of our business anyway.

So what's the godly response to someone who claims a bizarre calling from God? I'm not suggesting that we abandon all discernment. I am, however, suggesting that whatever our response is, it needs to come from our own current interaction with the Spirit of God, not from a mental blueprint of God's behavioral patterns. We need to pray about it and ask for discernment, offer counsel instead of opposition, ask questions that help the person affirm (or not) that the voice they heard was God's, and hold out for the possibility that even if we think it's unlikely, the person might actually be following God's will. When someone's obedience seems suspiciously quirky,

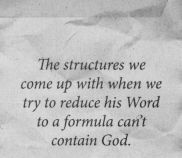

*The structures we come up with when we try to reduce his Word to a formula can't contain God.*

we need to realize that this is exactly how we would have perceived most people in the Bible if we knew them at the time. That doesn't mean that the claims we hear are always true; sometimes people really are off base. But it does mean that we can't express contempt for people's actions because they seem odd or because they stretch our understanding of what's appropriate. We have to find a better reason.

We also have to be open to the possibility that God might call us personally to an alarming task. If we're obsessed with our reputation in the community, we won't be able to answer. The fear of human opinions, scripturally and throughout history, is an enormous obstacle to obedience. God's image isn't always pleasing to religious minds. If we aren't open to his leading, especially when that leading might be offensive to others, we'll miss out on the blessing that comes by following him completely.

**FORGOTTEN MESSAGES FROM HOSEA:**
+ God sometimes violates our sense of propriety with a plan that we think couldn't possibly be his will.
+ God's plan sometimes supersedes the instructions or commandments he's already given us.
+ It is therefore impossible at times for us to follow the biblical patterns we normally follow and still obey the voice of God.

# CHAPTER 7

# PRIDE OR PREJUDICE?

**JASON (YOUTH MINISTER):** Okay, listen up to a few announcements: If you're planning to go on the ski retreat next weekend, I need a signed permission form from your parents by Wednesday. You can bring it to our pizza fellowship Wednesday night if you want. But I've got to have it by then. Also, if you even think you *might* want to go on the mission trip this summer, go ahead and sign up. It's not a commitment—it's just so we'll have a general idea of how many are interested. Okay, that's it for business. Now, let's go around the room for prayer requests, okay? Let's start with Emily and go to the left.

**EMILY:** My mom's still looking for a job. She wants something where she only has to work during school hours so she can be home when my little brother and I get home from school.

**JASON:** Okay, we'll pray for that. Ashley, what about you?

**ASHLEY:** Um, everything's okay right now. Maybe we can pray for exams in a couple of weeks.

**JASON:** Good idea. I'm sure everybody can relate to that. José, what's going on in your life that we can pray about?

**JOSÉ:** Well . . . my family hates me. I don't know how long I can live there.

**JASON:** I'm sure they don't really hate you, José.

**JOSÉ:** No, they do. They said so. I had this dream where I was their boss and they had to kneel down in front of me and do whatever I said. So when I told them about it, they got really mad and quit talking to me.

**ASHLEY:** Why would you tell them that, José?

**JASON**: Yeah, probably not a great idea.

**JOSÉ**: Well, anyway, I did. And now they hate me.

**JASON**: They'll come around. Once they realize that you must have dreamed that because maybe you're insecure in your relationship with them, they won't see it as an ego thing. Besides, it was just a dream.

**JOSÉ**: I told them I thought it was more than a dream—that God was going to bless me more than them.

**JASON**: Okay . . . so maybe it was an ego thing after all.

**EMILY**: I can't believe you had the nerve to say that.

**JASON**: Why would you think that, José?

**JOSÉ**: It was a very realistic dream, man. It was totally like I was there. Even my parents had to obey me.

**JASON**: I don't think God would tell you to think something disrespectful of your parents like that. We're supposed to honor our parents, not order them around. God's not going to contradict his own Word. Usually a vivid dream like this means you're really struggling with something underneath the surface. It looks to me like you feel some kind of need to get out from under your parents and your brothers. Have they been giving you a hard time?

**JOSÉ**: Kind of, but I don't think that's what it is. God spoke to people in dreams in the Bible, didn't he? So it's like that.

**EMILY**: Dreams aren't reality, José. Everybody has dreams. Most of them are just weird.

**ASHLEY**: Yeah, you can't base your life on something like that. You'd have to change direction every other day.

**JASON**: Not to mention that God doesn't really speak to people that way anymore. He did that in Bible times because they didn't have the Bible yet. Now he speaks to us through his Word. Plus, look at the fruit of this. Jesus said you'll know things by their fruit, and all this has done is get your family riled up against you. If it's bad fruit, then obviously it didn't come from God.

**JOSÉ:** Well, pray for me anyway. They're making my life miserable . . . I mean, more than usual.

**JASON:** Yeah, man, we'll do that. Mark, you're next. How are things in your world?

+ + + +

Joseph didn't have family values typical of modern evangelicalism. Actually, he might have *had* them, but his family certainly didn't exhibit them. His father, for example, was married to two women who engaged in competitive childbearing involving not only themselves but their maids, producing twelve sons and an unspecified number of daughters. Joseph's uncle had sought to murder his brother, Joseph's father, which is why Dad ended up back in the old country marrying those two women. Joseph's grandfather, the father of Dad's two wives, was a slick salesman with serious ethical shortcomings.

Joseph's brothers were sometimes split into opposing factions—the "real" sons vs. the maids' sons.[1] His sister had been raped, which sent two of his brothers on a killing spree that caused the family to have to leave town. And his mother, his dad's favored wife, died giving birth to his little brother. That meant Joseph's "favorite child" status became even more ingrained in his father, causing extreme animosity among his siblings and almost resulting in Joseph's death. Instead, his brothers "only" sold him into slavery with full intentions of never seeing him again. And later, one of his older brothers slept with his own daughter-in-law because he refused to provide children for her through more legitimate means, so she tricked him. Yes, Joseph came from one of the most dysfunctional families in recorded history.

The patriarchal stories are the ancient version of a soap opera, only these were the people God chose in order to reveal himself to the world. Considering this background, Joseph was remarkably free of neuroses. But he might have done some unwise things in his life, especially as a teenager. One of those things was telling his family that they would one day bow down to him. How did he know that? He had a dream—two versions, same message. The eleventh son of the family would be exalted above his ten older brothers and even his parents (though his mother had already died).

Opinions of Joseph's early life are split into two camps. One side sees him as an innocent son who would live a life highly symbolic of the Messiah himself. The other side sees him as an arrogant brat who flaunted his father's favor in front of the brothers who had more legitimate claims to receive the family's inheritance. The Bible doesn't really tell us which of these pictures fits Joseph best. It simply reports his behavior. But regardless of whether Joseph was good and naive or proud and boastful, one thing is clear: the implications of his dreams were shocking and offensive.

*The patriarchal stories are the ancient version of a soap opera, only these were the people God chose in order to reveal himself to the world.*

I don't think we grasp the blunt force of Joseph's dreams today. It isn't unusual in modern society for parents to give the biggest portion of their estate to one of their younger children or for a younger child to have higher ambitions than an older child—or, for that matter, for a child to disrespect parents and older siblings. But in ancient cultures—and in many modern ones outside of North America—families had a well-defined pecking order. It wasn't acceptable to usurp the place of one's elders, which Joseph's father, Jacob, knew all too well from his own experience. In fact, an eleventh son claiming higher status than his older brothers and even his father would be similar to a private telling a general and ten colonels they'd be taking orders from him one day, maybe soon. It was extremely disrespectful and rebellious. And from the way Joseph seemed to tell it, there wasn't necessarily a "one day" implication involved. He could easily have been saying—or they could have simply perceived him as saying—something along the lines of "God says I'm favored above you all, so you should bow down to me. Right now would be good." That's just rude.

In hindsight, of course, we know that God was behind Joseph's dreams and that those dreams would one day be fulfilled. But claiming God's endorsement up front didn't help matters very much. The Bible tells us that Joseph's brothers were angry and hated him all the more, but it doesn't report what they said. I can imagine, though, that if they could bring themselves to speak to him directly, they would have said things like, "God wouldn't tell you something that smacks of rebellion. His purposes bring peace and harmony in the home, and this obviously does the opposite, so it clearly isn't God's will. Your pride has so twisted your thinking that you're delusional. Besides, you can't rely on dreams anyway. You never can tell if it's God's guidance or a stomach full of rotten figs you ate the night before. You have to be discerning about dreams, and it's obvious that this one doesn't fit God's character at all. He told you to honor your parents, not force them to bow to you."

*I don't think we grasp the blunt force of Joseph's dreams today.*

If we were in the midst of Joseph's situation, or if he were in the midst of ours, we would want to bring him down a notch or two just like his brothers did. We'd be wrong, of course—Jesus made extravagant claims, too, and they had nothing to do with pride. They were truth, as Joseph's turned out to be. But we wouldn't know that when the words first came out of his mouth. We'd take a disliking to him instantly.

Don't believe me? Then imagine the first day of a discussion group when participants take turns introducing themselves to the leader and each other. It's always nice to share a little bit about oneself during those kinds of introductions, isn't it? So leaders often ask for a small nugget of your personality—something like, "Hi, my name is so-and-so, and what I hope to get out of this class is . . ." So imagine someone standing up when it's his turn and saying with a very serious expression, "Hi, my name is Joe, and I think God has given me a better grasp of this subject than the rest of you will ever have, so all of you can come to me for help if you need to." How do you feel about that group member? If you're another member, you think, *What a jerk!* And if you're the leader, you think, *Who does he think he is? I'm educated in this field and this is his first exposure to it!* Gets on your nerves, doesn't it?

Or imagine an intern telling a CEO and ten senior vice presidents that they would come crawling to him one day for a job because he's gifted enough to rise to the top quicker than they did. How well would that go over? The intern would be hoping to rise to the top in another company the next day.

The point is that any godly observer would probably look at Joseph's dreams as an attack on God's standards for families. And in the aftermath of negative reactions, hard feelings, bitter rivalries, and jockeying for position, any godly observer would be convinced that with such horrendous fruit, the tree couldn't be good. The evidence would be in the outcome. Provoking an entire family to such intense jealousy and murderous anger couldn't be God's will. That would divide the home, which is supposed to be a place of refuge for a loving family. It would be obvious that God wasn't blessing this grandiose plan.

So we'd try to fix Joseph by having a talk with his teachers, recommending him for counseling, and trying to teach his brothers about loving the unlovable and forgiving those who don't deserve it. And considering the degree of animosity, we might strongly encourage a period of separation so everyone could cool off. Then we'd pray really hard for God to deal firmly but lovingly with Joseph's arrogant attitude and teach him things like humility and respect. And while Joseph might really have needed such an approach, depending on how one interprets his early life, we'd completely miss the fact that the dreams were true and he was only being honest about what God said. Voicing that honesty out loud may not have been the wisest thing in the world, but it wasn't implicitly sinful. And Joseph's eventual rise in Egypt would turn out to be a key part of God's will for his people.

So once again, our "biblical" approach would oppose biblical truth and would counsel against God's purposes. Our ideals for family harmony would outweigh God's overriding purpose for that dysfunctional family. Our inability to see beyond the immediate in both time and circumstances would cause us to miss the big picture. And our expectations of what God is supposed to do would blind us to what he's actually doing. Our biblical worldview would eliminate one of the Bible's most respected heroes before he ever grew up.

> *Our expectations of what God is supposed to do sometimes blind us to what he's actually doing.*

Let me be clear that God supports families, hates pride, and loves deeply fulfilling relationships. But Romans

8:28 wasn't written for a perfect world. In working all things together for the good of those who love him, God has to factor in some pretty ugly junk. And sometimes that junk turns out to have been a critical part of his plan.

The contemporary church, generally speaking, has a false perception that God is not the author of confusion. Since that's basically a quote from 1 Corinthians 14:33, it's easy to see why most Christians think it's biblical. It's in the Bible. But one of our interpretations of it isn't in the Bible. This verse has nothing to do with everything going peacefully and smoothly. If that were the case, the day of Pentecost in Acts 2 was certainly not from God, nor was Paul's trip to Ephesus in Acts 19. Those were extremely chaotic and disordered events. But the Holy Spirit was behind both of them, as well as many others, so we know that's not what Paul's statement to the Corinthians was about. He was referring to worship services that had turned into a kind of competitive chatter that no one could understand or learn from, and in which no clear authority was recognized. That, he said, is not characteristic of God's Spirit. But the disorder and confusion that result from the Holy Spirit stepping into our agendas and making a scene? That's another story altogether.

We see this not only in Acts but also throughout church history. The Protestant Reformation threw Europe into social unrest, political confusion, periodic warfare, and religious conflict for well over a century. Was it from God? Any non-Catholic, non-Orthodox Christian today would either have to say it was or become a self-contradiction. The First Great Awakening in the United States during the eighteenth century was considered by some to be "only temporary," "superficial," and even "evil." One historian notes, "Conservative and moderate clergymen questioned the emotionalism of evangelicals and charged that disorder and discord attended the revivals."[2] The Welsh Revival of 1904–05 was judged for similar transgressions. "Spontaneity and seeming disorder replaced promotion, scheduling, regular preaching, financial planning, and even systematic evangelistic outreach."[3] In fact, nearly every revival movement has drawn sharp criticism for excessive emotionalism, superficiality, divisiveness, chaos, and gross theological error. Yet historically, these revivals have brought multitudes to Christ and changed the face of Christian churches and denominations. Clearly, God's work often comes in untidy packaging.

So our idea that God is not at work in a situation unless it's harmonious, joyful, and calm is not a biblical perspective. It's one of those attempts to get God to fit our expectations. Sometimes he does—I'm a big fan of harmony, joy, and peace—but often he doesn't. And divisions and hostility that may erupt because people react negatively to God's voice have little bearing on whether God actually gave direction or not. Sometimes his guidance gets exactly that response, and sometimes it doesn't. Sometimes it defies social conventions and offends religious sensibilities, and sometimes it doesn't. And sometimes the words and behavior that stir up controversy really are ungodly, but sometimes they aren't. Harsh or divisive reactions aren't valid criteria for determining God's will. We have to be in communication with his Spirit to find the truth of a matter.

> *Godly people may be called to do or say things that ruffle a lot of feathers and make it look as if they're the problem.*

When someone stands at the center of self-inflicted chaos and dysfunction, don't assume all the tumult springs out of some form of ungodliness or disobedience. Godly people with the right perspective can still be called to do or say things that ruffle a lot of feathers and make it look as if they're the problem. God himself is holy and pure, yet he stands in the midst of controversy and even instigates it from time to time. That's because when truth inserts itself into a context of misperceptions and brokenness, the short-term outcome can get really unpleasant. But the long-term outcome can be beautiful, if in fact God authored the situation or chooses to redeem it. And in Joseph's case, he did.

### FORGOTTEN MESSAGES FROM JOSEPH:

+ Sometimes God's will causes chaos, confusion, and bitterness. When we try to discern a tree by its fruit, we need to take into account the messiness of hearing and obeying his voice. Even the best-tasting fruit doesn't always look good on the tree.
+ God's purposes are not hindered by soap-opera-level dysfunction.
+ God doesn't always adhere strictly to family protocol, even when the family protocol is something he authored in the first place.

# CHAPTER 8

# THE SCANDAL
# ON THE FLOOR

"Hey, Bo, can I talk to you for a minute?"

"Sure, Carl, what's up?"

"I heard you're planning to get married. Congratulations."

"Thanks, man. I was hoping you'd consider being one of my grooms-men. What do you think?"

"Wow, Bo, I'd be honored. Thanks. I just . . . well, as a friend, I just wanted to make sure she's the right girl for you. I want you to be happy, and . . ."

"Oh, you heard about the proposal."

"Yeah. I just don't want you to feel pressured to do this unless you're positive about her. I hate to say this, but . . . have you considered that maybe she's just . . ."

"Using me to get her green card? Yeah, I know it looks that way. But I love her, Carl. And I know she's the real thing. I know she loves me too."

"Okay, that's cool. It just seems a little . . . I don't want you to be offended, but I'm sure you realize how this looks. She's a beautiful, young immigrant, and you're a successful, middle-aged businessman. She's needy and a new believer, and you're stable, respectable, mature, and . . . just the kind of man who makes a great catch for a foreigner who wants citizenship. And then when I heard you got engaged—well, *she* practical-ly proposed to *you*, you know? To be honest, I'm worried that she's just in it for the benefits and will end up breaking your heart."

"I appreciate your concern, Carl, but trust me. I know her well enough to know she's not like that. I realize it looks a little unconven-tional, but we're in love. It'll last."

"Okay, I'll trust you. I guess I'm worried because I know how sym-pathetic you are toward people who are going through a tough time, and it's possible for someone compassionate like you to want so much to rescue her that your feelings could look a lot like real love. But then once you've rescued her, will there be enough there to build a marriage on? You could feel stuck. I'd hate to see you save the day for her at the expense of your own desires. I know how long you've looked for a wife who fits you perfectly."

"But she does, Carl. That's the beauty of it. Sure, she has needs, but it's like God brought to my doorstep the one person who was designed specifically for me."

"All right, then. If you're sure. But please reassure me about one thing. Toby said he heard a rumor that you and she . . . um, I'm not sure how to say this, 'cause I don't want to question your integrity. And I don't . . . it's just that I don't know her very well, and she can probably be pretty persuasive with her looks . . ."

"No, Carl, I didn't sleep with her, if that's what you're trying to ask. Someone else asked me that too—thought she must have seduced me and now I feel obligated to her. That's just . . . that's not what happened. She wouldn't do that. *I* wouldn't do that."

"I know, I didn't think so. I'm sorry to even mention it. But I'm relieved to hear you say it anyway. Everyone can be tempted, right? Honestly, I wouldn't have asked except that I'm just concerned for you. You're a good friend."

+ + + +

Ruth was a foreigner. Not just any foreigner, but a Moabite—a native of a country that Israelites practically equated with gross immorality. Long ago in Genesis, Lot and his two daughters had fled Sodom as it was being destroyed and found refuge in a cave. Realizing that their prospects of having children were considerably damaged by Sodom's demise—their fiancés had died in the destruction—the daughters came up with a plan. They would get their father drunk on successive nights and take turns sleeping with him. Their plan worked, they each got pregnant, and the older daughter bore a son named Moab. And all Moabites, including Ruth, inherited the stigma of that sordid, incestuous affair.

As the book of Ruth opens, an Israelite woman named Naomi who is living in Moab has recently suffered the loss of her husband and two sons. Her two young daughters-in-law are both Moabites and now widows. Lacking any family support structure in Moab, Naomi decides to return to Judah. Ruth insists on coming with her and making a new life in her deceased husband's homeland. She abandons the gods of Moab to attach herself to Israel and Israel's God.

But Ruth was childless when her husband died, and she can't really be grafted into the nation of Israel without bearing Israelite children. She needs a new husband from her dead husband's extended family. And for some reason, she's drawn to an older gentleman named Boaz. He's financially comfortable, well respected, and very kind to her. She probably hasn't received much mercy in Israel yet; she's an alien from the land of corruption, obviously cursed by her gods since her husband was taken from her at such a young age. But Boaz notices her hard work in the fields and hears the story of her faithfulness to Naomi and Israel's God. She might have been harmed in other fields, Naomi tells her, but Boaz's field is safe. She feels the warmth of his kindness.

Naomi comes up with a plan to plant a suggestion in Boaz's mind to marry Ruth. It involves some boldness on Ruth's part, both to go to him in the middle of the night and to initiate her own marriage. But Ruth is up to the challenge and even takes it a step further. In a passage that uses quite a bit of innuendo to suggest the sexual tension in the situation, Ruth uncovers Boaz and asks him to spread his garment over her.[1] She even appeals to Deuteronomic laws of remarriage, making it clear what her intentions are. This is a bona fide marriage proposal.

Though we can assume that no immorality occurred on the threshing floor in the middle of the night, the book of Ruth is a rather racy story for the time and culture in which it was written. There are echoes of Ruth's ancestry—a young woman approaching an older man in his sleep after he's had a lot to drink, just as Lot's daughters once did—as well as a stretching of current cultural norms. It isn't hard to imagine a roomful of ancient Jews launching into a debate after reading or hearing this story: "Did Ruth sin in what she did?"

*The book of Ruth is a rather racy story for the time and culture in which it was written.*

"No, she never had sex with him until after they were married . . . I think."

"There are other kinds of sin involved. She put both of them in a very tempting situation and left them open to all kinds of speculation. That in itself is sinful."

"It may not have been sinful, but it certainly wasn't wise."

"Well, what about him? Boaz should have gotten up and fled the situation. That's what Joseph did in Potiphar's house in Genesis. Flee immorality. But Boaz stuck around and even let her sleep there the rest of the night!"

"Yeah, but he just wanted to make sure she wasn't on the road at night."

"But what if the other guys woke up and saw her there early in the morning? What a bad example for them."

And on and on it would go. Except the story of Ruth is a fantastic picture of salvation, with Boaz being the Christ-figure and Ruth representing those of us from any background who are needy and desperate for a redeemer. It's also a God-inspired story, a real-life parable of his heart for his people. Godly people of any age, if they understood the nuances, would experience real tension between what they knew to be God's law and what they read in this story. It just doesn't look like something God would approve of.

Imagine Ruth in an accountability group for single women. What would the members say to her?

"Ruth, it's the man's job to pursue and the woman's to play hard-to-get. That way you weed out the guys who aren't serious about a relationship from the one who's deeply in love with you. This is how God designed us. You can't just throw yourself at a man like that."

"Yeah, that just reeks of immodesty. Brazen seduction. He may have been flattered, but he won't trust you later."

"Do you know what people think when they see a young woman with an older man? Do you really want to go through life with all those raised eyebrows around you? And if you have kids, think about how old he'll be when they're teenagers."

"You're leaving yourself open to all kinds of gossip with that kind of behavior."

"Not even a hint of immorality, Ruth. Not even a hint. You should know better than that."

In all of our advice, of course, we'd miss out on the redemptive heart of God. The picture of boldly coming to Christ for our salvation, no matter the cost to our reputation, would be lost on us. The beauty of an exciting romance that mirrors God's compassion and love would be overshadowed by the scandalous implications. No actual sin occurred in this romance, but hints of impropriety certainly did. And when we see hints of impropriety, issues of righteousness take center stage. All other issues—like God's merciful, affectionate heart—are ignored.

We are able to see the real meaning of the story of Ruth today because it has the approval of the Holy Spirit as part of sacred Scripture and because we can see the redemptive pictures in it. But I'm convinced we wouldn't have that sense of appreciation if Ruth was playing at the local theater and we weren't already familiar with the story.

One of my major goals in life is to develop the kind of heart that recognizes the voice and the movements of God at first sight rather than figuring out it was him after he's already passed by. I don't want a system of beliefs that only acknowledges God's work in history but doesn't expect him to work today. I want the kind of theology that allows him to unfold his stories right in front of my eyes without my beating the life out of them with questions and skepticism and judgments. I'm determined not to be the type of believer who honors the prophets in hindsight but would have thrown rocks at them in their time. That's the history of Israel and, to be honest, most of the church. But that's not the kind of faith God honors with his presence and power.

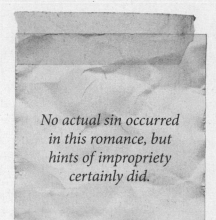

*No actual sin occurred in this romance, but hints of impropriety certainly did.*

No, God honors the kind of faith that Clarence Jordan had in establishing Koinonia Farm in south Georgia in the 1940s as a racially integrated community with Sermon on the Mount ethics. That's radical and bold. At that time and place, the biblical principles of Jordan's vision were considered by many Christians to be decidedly unbiblical and even sinful. So some of the fine Christians who opposed him decided to respond

*God honors Ruth's kind of faith—honest, sacrificial, risky, bold, unconventional.*

with bombings and other acts of violence—in the name of God, of course, just as certain priests and teachers condemned Jesus to die for the sake of protecting God's chosen people from both heresy and the wrath of Rome. Jordan had Kingdom faith, which almost always draws sniper attacks from those who can't differentiate between the Kingdom of God and the kingdom in their own head.

And God honors Ruth's kind of faith—honest, sacrificial, risky, bold, unconventional. We know he honors it because her story is in the Bible. She became the great-grandmother of King David and a member of the lineage of Jesus. Whenever we get too judgmental about someone who appears "inappropriate," we should remember that the Messiah's genealogy wouldn't have looked the same if Ruth hadn't cast aside her stigmas and lain next to a man in the middle of the night.

### FORGOTTEN MESSAGES FROM RUTH:

+ Not all that appears inappropriate actually is.
+ God speaks to us in the parables of real-life situations—ours and those of the people around us.
+ God's romantic heart beats faster than we think.
+ God will make a statement about his love, even if it might result in gossip and disapproval. He's not afraid of a scandal with a purpose.
+ Sometimes the immigrants among us—those whose culture and habits look ungodly to us and/or whom we wish our government would handle better—are more spiritually mature and have greater faith than we do.

# CHAPTER 9

# SURE, SHE'S A VIRGIN

One day at a Christian crisis pregnancy center, a young woman named Maria comes in for a pregnancy test. And the volunteer counselor, who has heard it all before, finds out that she really hasn't heard anything quite like this.

"Hi, Maria. Come on in. My name is Amy. What brings you in today?"

"Well, I wanted to see if I could get a pregnancy test. I know I'm going to get pregnant, but maybe I already am. I just wanted to check."

"Sure, we can help you with that. So this is a planned pregnancy?"

"No . . . um, actually, yes. I mean, not by me."

"You mean someone is pushing you into it?"

"Yes . . . or no, not exactly . . . I don't mind. It's good. It's kind of hard to explain."

"Don't be nervous, okay? Just relax; we're here to help. We can talk about that some more later if you like. Have you been here before?"

"No, never."

"Okay, you'll need to fill out some paperwork that will help us get to know you a little better. If you want, we can go over it together and fill it out as we talk, okay?"

"Sure."

"Can we get your last name, or would you prefer not to?"

"Just Maria's good."

"Okay, that's fine. And how old are you?"

"I'm sixteen."

"All right. Yeah, I think it's a little early for you to be trying to get pregnant. But if you already are, don't worry. We'll help you deal with that. Now, when was your last period?"

"It's been about five weeks."

"Five weeks? That's not very late, Maria."

"I know, but like I said, it's going to happen. I'm just a little anxious to find out when."

"Okay, well, let's finish with the paperwork and then I think we have some things to talk about. Tell me about your partner, or partners. Don't be embarrassed. Are you in a relationship?"

"You mean with a man?"

"Yes, sweetie, a man."

"I'm engaged. I'm sure I'll get pregnant soon."

"Well, that's probably true if you continue to have sex and aren't using any birth control. You know what they say: if you shoot at the target long enough, you'll eventually hit the bull's-eye. Of course, we believe God's plan is to wait until after the wedding to have intimate relations with your husband."

"Oh, yes! I do too."

"You do? Maria, something's not adding up here. You know you have to have intercourse to get pregnant, right? I'm assuming you and your fiancé have talked about family planning."

"Sort of. Not in those exact words, but we've talked."

"Then how do you think you're going to get pregnant?"

"God told me I would."

"Um, okay. Well, I do believe he still speaks, so I'm sure it's possible he may have promised you that. But that's real subjective, Maria. It's hard to recognize his voice. And he usually doesn't tell us when these things will happen. Don't you think when it happens it will be like everyone else? After you and your fiancé have gotten married and spent a little time together as a couple—and *then* you start your family?"

"No, God said I would get pregnant first, then we'd get married, then I'd have the baby, and then we can be intimate."

"Oh, Maria, honey, it just doesn't happen that way. I don't think God would have told you something like that. How did you think you heard him?"

"It was very clear. He sent an angel to tell me I would conceive by his Spirit."

"Are you sure that was God, Maria?"

"Yes, of course. Who else would it be?"

"Maria, don't be offended, but I have to ask you a few questions. Have you heard other voices before?"

"No, not like this."

"And have you received any counseling, or maybe talked to a psychiatrist before about some problems you've been having?"

"No, not at all."

"Okay. And have you been taking any medications?"

"No."

"Are you sure? Any experimenting, like some girls your age do?"

"No, of course not. I wouldn't do that."

"It's all right if you have. We're not here to judge."

"No, I promise."

"Maria, I have to tell you, I'm a bit concerned. I want you to be very honest with me. Has anyone ever abused you, maybe assaulted you sexually? If you're ashamed or trying to deny what has happened, don't worry about that here. There's absolutely no reason to feel ashamed. I've heard all kinds of stories in these rooms—you can be totally open."

"Honestly, nothing like that has happened. I've never come in contact with a man that way. Not even close."

"Hmm. Let's see, Maria . . . maybe this will help: we'll go ahead and do the test for you, and when it comes back negative, let's talk about why you might be so focused on this idea of conceiving before you have intercourse, okay?"

Later:

"Well, Maria, you were right. It's positive. I've been thinking about what you've told me, and I think I see what's going on. You and your fiancé have had a pure relationship, but someone recently molested you and now you're terrified that your fiancé will find out the truth and call off the wedding. So you've developed this story that clears you from anything immoral and explains your pregnancy at the same time. But, sweetie, listen to me. Your fiancé won't fall for that. He just isn't going to believe it. No man would."

"No, that's not it at all. That's not what happened. No one raped me or anything."

"Maria, it's not your fault. There's nothing to be ashamed of. This kind of thing happens, and it's tragic. I know how devastating it can be.

My heart breaks for you. But you're still a beautiful, pure daughter of God. That's how he sees you, no matter what. And it doesn't do anyone any good to try to protect whoever did this. If it's a family member or a friend, I know that can be really hard. But you have to tell the truth, or he might end up doing that to someone else someday."

"You don't understand. No one did anything against my will. It was God. I've told my fiancé already, and he believes me. God told him the same thing too."

"Maria . . . um . . . well, okay, I'm not qualified to counsel you about these kinds of things . . . but I really do want you to ask God to help you see his perspective on it. The sooner you can deal with what happened, the sooner you can begin to heal and get on with your life. Okay, so much for my speech. Let's get practical. What we do now—and we do this for everyone who tests positive, even if they know what they want to do—is let you watch an educational video. It will show you the stages of development of your baby and give you some information about things to avoid. Obviously, since we're a Christian agency, we want you to be fully informed about abortion and know what the risks and dangers are—not just physically, but emotionally and spiritually too. So just be forewarned that the video frankly discusses that."

"Really, I don't think this is necessary. I know what I'm going to do."

"Are you sure? Because it has some good information about prenatal care too."

"Okay, I guess that would be good."

"All right, before we watch, let me just ask you a few more questions. You said you weren't on any medications, including birth control pills, right?"

"Right."

"Great. That's good. It's very important to stay off of medications during your pregnancy unless your doctor prescribes them and monitors them for you. Now let's talk about your support network. Do you have family members who will be supportive?"

"Not really."

"Have you thought about how your parents might react?"

"I'm not sure. They won't kill me, but I don't think I can count on them accepting this. I think they'll be really ashamed of me."

"Any brothers or sisters or other family members who will support you?"

"I have a cousin I'm really close to. She doesn't live in town, though. But I'll probably go visit her. She and I have kind of a connection."

"Good. So it sounds like you have at least a few people to depend on. And your fiancé—sounds like he's supportive. What about his family? Do you think they'll try to pressure you not to have the child?"

"Not have it? No, I don't think so. I don't think they would ever approve of an abortion."

"Okay, that's good. But will they be accepting of your child? Having the help of the birth father's family is huge."

"I don't think they'll want to be involved. They won't want me to get an abortion, but I'm sure they'll still be really embarrassed by this."

"So other than your fiancé and one cousin, you don't really have anyone to turn to?"

"No. I think the two of us may need to move somewhere else and start fresh."

"Maria, I'm at a loss for how to help you. Of course, you can go through our clothes closet and get some maternity clothes, and in the ninth month you can come back and get some clothes for your baby. I'm going to give you my card, and I want you to keep it somewhere where you can find it. I really hope you'll consider letting us help you with an adoption plan. I know you don't see that as an option right now, but hang on to my card just in case. Promise?"

"Okay, sure."

"Please take care, Maria. Let us know how we can help. God bless you."

+ + + +

The nativity story is one of the most beautiful in all of religious literature. To us, it's more than beautiful; it's sacred. It's the record of how God incarnated his Son into this world to save us. We're inspired by Mary's faith and devotion and impressed with the hardship she went through for the privilege of being Jesus' mother. We also respect Joseph's faithful stewardship of his calling to quietly be the earthly father to God's Son. And, of course, the birth event itself—the manger scene, the star, the shepherds in the field, the wise men, the angels singing—every December, we commemorate that unique and special advent. Christmas speaks powerfully to us still.

Sometimes lost on us is the stunning way in which God clothed himself in human flesh. It's easy to be sympathetic toward Mary and get angry at the people who would have tried to stone her if they knew she was pregnant. But have you ever considered how you'd respond to a teenage girl who became pregnant and then said God did it? Even with the biblical precedent of Jesus' conception and the annual reminder of it at Christmas, we still wouldn't think it was true. We'd be right, of course—the Incarnation was a once-in-an-eternity event. But imagine being a real person in real history in the real culture of Mary and Joseph. Imagine how ludicrous it must have sounded. "I'm pregnant, but it's okay; I'm still a virgin!" Only divine intervention would convince us that there was a remote possibility of that being true. In all honesty, we have to admit that we'd assume the worst and, in fact, judge Mary more for the lie than for the immorality.

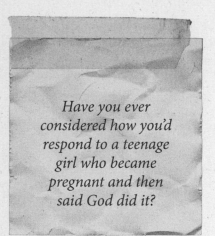

*Have you ever considered how you'd respond to a teenage girl who became pregnant and then said God did it?*

It's a wild story, and the only reason we believe it wasn't a fabrication is the proof of Jesus as God's Son years later. But the people who knew the young Mary, even her own family members, didn't see the end of the story. They had never heard Jesus teach or seen him heal. They had no framework that would cause them to say, "Yes, God must have done this wonderful thing!" It was undoubtedly a very traumatic, very contentious, and even very demeaning episode in Mary's life. The only thing that could have sustained her was the absolute certainty that God was the Author of this plan.

The counsel we would have given Mary, assuming we were not among the mockers and judgers, would have ranged from sympathetic pleas to stern rebukes. We would have told her just to own up to the truth and confess she'd slipped, to put the baby up for adoption into a nice Jewish family, to repent of her immorality, to insist that Joseph marry her or at least agree to pay child support, to realize that a crisis couldn't be covered up with a fantasy explanation, and so on. The one thing we would *not* have said to her is, "Wow, how amazing that you get to be the mother of the Messiah!"

It's fascinating to me that months before God incarnate came to us in the clothes of humility and simplicity, he came to us in the clothes of apparent immorality. He knew full well that a young woman claiming to be pregnant by the Holy Spirit would be nearly universally greeted with skepticism and derision. Much of her family and most of her friends surely believed she was lying, no matter how spotless her character had always been. A virgin birth is about as unbelievable as a resurrection. Our minds can't accept such absurdities unless there's overwhelming evidence to convince us. And there would be a long thirty years between the mysterious birth and any impressive public evidence that this child was more than simply human. So Mary would have been under suspicion for behaving immorally and for trying to cover it up for three decades before being vindicated—and even then, the vindication was unconvincing to those who weren't inclined to believe.[1] Mary bore the stigma of having an illegitimate son for a long time—at least among the few who were privy to the story in the first place.

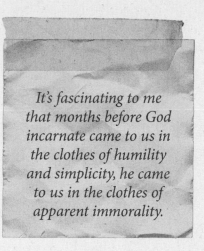

*It's fascinating to me that months before God incarnate came to us in the clothes of humility and simplicity, he came to us in the clothes of apparent immorality.*

It would be easy at this point to say, "So what? This event isn't repeatable. I'm not ever going to have to believe God about something this absurd." And if we're talking about this specific situation, that's true. But we have no guarantees that God won't bring other bizarre situations into our lives. In fact, he may already have done so; we just didn't recognize his work because we ruled out the possibility of it being from him as soon as we heard it. If God is the same now as he was then—and obviously, he is—then it's entirely possible that he would work in someone's life in other highly unlikely ways. And there aren't many people today who would echo Mary's obedience.

Think of her response when Gabriel told her the news: "May it be done to me according to your word" (Luke 1:38). That simple faith in God's plan came before she could even begin to understand the plan, before she thought of the reaction people might have, before any signs of confirmation were shown, before the impossible details could even settle into her mind, and before she could figure out how to maintain a good reputation. The absurdity, the appearance of immorality, the scandal and disgrace, the stones that might be thrown at her, the husband who might reject her, the stigma she might have to live with the rest of her life, the isolation from the community of faith—none of these really mattered. When God speaks, everything else is a minor detail.

> *When God speaks, everything else is a minor detail.*

That's the attitude we need to have if we want God to do miraculous things in our lives. Our miracles won't always come in clean packages. They can be really messy sometimes, even scandalous. They can stretch the faith and imagination of other believers so thin that an explosion is sure to happen. And when it does, we'd better be prepared to press ahead in spite of the hostility that surely will come against us. Many people will get downright judgmental, assuming that our Christian lingo is a mask to keep others from seeing our real issues. And even if others can see that God is up to something good, they often don't like any hint that would indicate God's favor on someone other than themselves. But when God speaks, the reactions of others are irrelevant. The absurdity of his words are no indication that they aren't his.

Not only do we need to have Mary's attitude in our own dealings with God, we also need to give other people the room to hear his voice in unpredictable and absurd ways too. Why should God's servants suffer the rejection of their own brothers and sisters in Christ simply because they hear his voice and believe it? Are we really so out of sync with the Holy Spirit that his true acts don't resonate within us when we encounter them in someone else?

Consider these scenarios:

+ A student says God helped her write a paper so well that it could easily be mistaken for an excerpt from a doctoral dissertation. But she promises she didn't plagiarize.

+ A missionary realizes there's not enough food for the crowd that came to hear a famous speaker, so he goes away for a few minutes and comes back with fifty loaves of bread. But he swears that God miraculously multiplied a couple of loaves that were still in his car—in spite of the fact that he was gone long enough to visit the neighborhood bakery.

+ A man buys a mountain in South America from a mining company because he's convinced that gold will be discovered there. He claims no inside information, no leak of proprietary knowledge. Instead, he was simply following a prophecy given to him at a church. A few months later, he's the richest man around, and he's using his wealth to bankroll Christian work around the country.

> *Why should God's servants suffer the rejection of their own brothers and sisters in Christ simply because they hear his voice and believe it?*

Impropriety could easily be assumed in each of these situations, which were drawn from testimonies of people I know personally. They're all true stories.[2] Nothing unethical or misleading was involved in any of them. In each case, a skeptic would focus on the opportunity for deception and a believer would take the testimony of supernatural help at face value. And that's always the way it is with a miracle; God rarely makes it so indisputably clear that the choice between faith and disbelief is obvious to us. He leaves a degree of ambiguity in it so we'll have to choose out of the leanings of our heart.

Mary chose to believe, in contrast to the high priest Zacharias a few verses earlier, who found himself in a similar situation and expressed his doubts. He was given the opportunity to repent later, and the two children who resulted from these mysterious events changed the world forever. One announced the Kingdom of God, and the other rode in as King. That's what faith leads to—even when it looks scandalous up front.

## FORGOTTEN MESSAGES FROM MARY:

+ When God clothed himself in human flesh, he clothed himself in scandalous circumstances.
+ The most far-fetched, flimsy denial of bad behavior might actually be true.
+ God sometimes waits several decades to vindicate his children's faith.

# CHAPTER 10

# BAD COMPANY

"I usually use my column in this magazine as an opportunity to highlight a great ministry that needs some exposure. But what I saw last week when David Lyons spoke at our annual denominational meeting was so symptomatic of the church's problems that I have to speak out.

Now, don't get me wrong. I think Rev. Lyons is a great speaker, and he certainly knows how to motivate a crowd. I'm not like those who are put off by his bluntness; I appreciate his ability to be direct, and I think it's healthy for American Christianity. No, it's what goes on behind the scenes that bothers me.

To put it bluntly—in the manner of Rev. Lyons, no less—he's a hypocrite. He talks about righteousness constantly, but he doesn't display it in his own life. It's not my place to speak to what's in his heart; that's between him and God. But he at least gives the appearance of casual morals, which the Bible explicitly warns us against doing. Christians are called to be "above reproach." Period. And Rev. Lyons isn't.

Let me give you a couple of examples. As a member of the media, I get an inside look into some of these events, and last week I got to observe Rev. Lyons's entourage for almost a full day. What I saw was alarming, to say the least. First, on the way to the convention floor from the parking lot, I saw a "lady"—and I use the term loosely, if you know what I mean—approaching us. Remember, now, the convention center isn't in the classiest part of town, just like any downtown area of a major city; and this woman was wearing some pretty suggestive clothing. I don't know what her occupation was, but I can guess. And all of a sudden, she ran up to Rev. Lyons, threw her arms around him, and said, "Dave! Thank you sooooo much for everything you've done for me. How can I ever repay you?" Then she hung on to him as if her life depended on it.

Now let's assume for a moment that her gratitude was for something entirely legitimate—some act of ministry or mercy he had done for her. Let's ignore the fact that she not only used his first name, but a very familiar form of his first name suggesting they were old friends (or worse). We'll give him the benefit of the doubt for now. Even so, what would any other respectable, high-profile minister do? He would gracefully remove himself from that suggestive situation and call some of his female associates—and there were plenty there—to come and minister to the woman's needs. But Lyons didn't do that. He allowed a person of very questionable morals to cling to him tightly and say some very personal things to him. That reeks of immorality.

That was what happened on the way to the podium that night, but there's more. He gave a rousing sermon, saw only a handful of people walk out, received a standing ovation from everyone who remained, and left behind him an enthusiastic crowd of this country's finest ministers. And then—in the dark of night—he went to dinner with a city councilman, whom I'll leave unnamed, where he and his entourage feasted on an extravagant, sumptuous meal and, from what I could see (and it was later confirmed to me by other sources), the wine flowed freely late into the night.

In case you're wondering, I don't enjoy being a snitch. That's not my role as a Christian journalist, and it never will be. I do, however, have a passion for the church's reputation. I think Christians should demonstrate that we have higher moral standards than anyone on the planet. Our purity should be visible to all. And as the Word says, there should never be even a *hint* of immorality among us. But with Rev. Lyons, there's so much more than a hint.

For that reason, I'm encouraging our denomination's leadership to avoid any future association with Rev. Lyons's ministry. Yes, he gives us a much-needed kick in the pants every once in a while, but at what cost? Our strong reputation in the evangelical community and in American society in general has been built piece by piece over many, many decades. I'd hate to see it tainted by one loose cannon who just happened to be invited to our annual convention. Considering some of the scandals that have rocked our fellow denominations in recent years, we need to view our reputation as a vital component of our witness. It's the only way the world will see what it means to rise above a sinful, futile way of life.

I truly pray that Rev. Lyons will clean up his act one day. I believe God can still use him to reach many. Just not here. Not with our folks. And certainly not at the expense of our hard-earned reputation."

+ + + +

I still remember the youth leader's question: "If Jesus came today, would you accept him?" *Of course,* I thought. *Why wouldn't I? I'd see his miracles and hear his teaching and accept him for the same reasons I already have.* Now, years later, I'm not so sure.

What changed my mind? Years of discipleship, I think, with a dash of seminary thrown in. Over time I've gotten the message that certain behaviors are unbecoming of Christians in public. I've been well trained in the principles of what it means to be Christlike, and when I look at Jesus . . . well, he doesn't quite fit.

Let me explain. We have a great understanding of many of the characteristics of Jesus, and we even know how to live some of them out. But in many respects, our knowledge of his attributes doesn't translate into the ways he put those attributes into practice. For example, we all know that Jesus was (and is) compassionate, so we set out to be compassionate too. But our definition of compassion doesn't always line up with his—like when he was declaring woes upon hypocritical teachers and scribes. Did Jesus not have compassion for them? Or was a direct confrontation the most compassionate thing he could do for them, perhaps the only approach that could shock some of them out of their complacency? I think it was the latter (in addition to being a compassionate defense of weary victims of false burdens). So while we understand the fact that Jesus is full of compassion, we don't always express that characteristic very accurately.

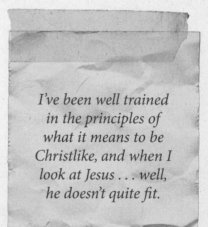

*I've been well trained in the principles of what it means to be Christlike, and when I look at Jesus . . . well, he doesn't quite fit.*

That particular example isn't very controversial, but plenty of others are, as the fictitious columnist above demonstrates. We've derived some pretty high standards from Scripture. For instance, I've always been taught that Christians should never allow themselves to be seen in any situation in which someone could potentially assume (incorrectly, of course) that they're abusing alcohol or engaging in any sort of inappropriate relationship. Not only should Christians keep their minds and hearts pure, their outward appearances should also make it clear that their minds and hearts are pure. In addition, I've learned that someone who is always at the center of controversy (1) doesn't know how to get along with people, (2) has a divisive personality, (3) gets a perverse kick out of stirring up trouble, or (4) is in desperate need of attention and only knows one way to get it. And when people make grandiose claims about their own plans and abilities, they're operating out of a spirit of pride and are likely compensating for deep, self-absorbing insecurities.

I think anyone who believes even half of the statements in that last paragraph would reject Jesus. He doesn't fit the picture of a sincere and faithful Christian very well. In all of our construction of what true discipleship should look like, we've come up with some pretty specific descriptions of what's Christlike and what isn't. And in the process, we've developed higher standards than Jesus had. We've fenced the gospel with lots of extra rules and expectations.

Consider our unstated definitions of godliness:

*Don't spend too much time with ungodly people, or you'll start acting like them.* Really? That would have turned Jesus into the glutton and drunkard many Jews accused him of being, a ladies' man much too comfortable with professional escorts, a man's man with lots of rough edges and vulgar tendencies, an insider with connections in an organized extortion ring (the corrupt tax system of the time), and so on.

But Jesus spent a lot of time with these outcasts and wasn't corrupted. "Yes, but he was incorruptible," you might say, and I agree that he had a certain advantage over us in the temptation department. But he *was* confronted with very real temptations,[1] and he withstood the tests. Not only that, he now fills us with his Holy Spirit, who, it should be pointed out, is *holy*. We can certainly give in to temptation, but we don't have to. The Spirit within us is greater than the spirit that would try to cause all of the sin around us to rub off on us. In fact, there's plenty of scriptural evidence that our purity can impact others more than their impurity impacts us.[2]

Jesus demonstrated this principle very graphically. In Old Testament law, a leper was sentenced to life in isolation outside the camp or city until his or her leprosy healed—which wasn't very often. This prohibition only made sense; leprosy can be quite contagious. Whoever comes into contact with it is at high risk of getting it. But then Jesus came along and touched lepers at the very site of their sores, and it wasn't the leprosy that rubbed off on him—it was his cleanness that rubbed off on them. In the natural realm, corruption spreads to what is pure. In the supernatural realm, purity can spread to what is corrupt. When a Christian is living a supernatural life, sin isn't the threat it used to be. It is good to be cautious, especially in areas in which we have a history of weakness. But afraid? Never. And certainly not governed by the expectations others have of us in these situations.

*In the natural realm, corruption spreads to what is pure. In the supernatural realm, purity can spread to what is corrupt.*

*"Among you there must not be even a hint of sexual immorality, or of any kind of impurity"* (Ephesians 5:3, NIV). Since this is a direct quote from the Bible, it shouldn't enter into this discussion of false ideals, should it? But there's a reason I quoted this particular translation of the verse: it's not quite accurate—at least not in the sense we often understand it. We've taken this verse and created a standard higher than the standard Jesus used for himself. We read this as "Do nothing that might give anyone the impression that you might be involved in any inappropriate relationship." That's generally wise advice, but it's not what this verse means—obviously, since Jesus violated it often by allowing women with bad reputations to speak to him in familiar terms and even touch him. Any kind of male-female contact in that culture would have been strictly governed and, unless among family members, usually forbidden. The fact that Jesus sat and talked with an immoral woman in public without shame or apology[3] and let an immoral woman spread her tears and perfume over his feet with her hair and kisses,[4] among other suspicious tolerations, makes a mockery of our interpretation of this verse and others like it.[5]

When Paul wrote those words, he was addressing the presence of actual sin in the congregation and imploring believers not to disgrace themselves with any vestige of immorality. More precise translations of this verse say not to let such sin "be named among you," in the sense that committing actual sin misrepresents the Spirit of God in his people. That's not the same as saying you should "never allow anyone to think you might possibly have had an opportunity to sin." We need to remember that we have little control over what gossips and slanderers say or even perceive. First-century Romans thought Christians practiced cannibalism because of all their talk about eating Christ's body and drinking his blood in the Lord's Supper, and nowhere in Scripture do we find any instructions to these believers to stop talking that way or participating in their "love feasts." Outsiders will always cast aspersions on believers— that's a common social dynamic in any area of life—and we aren't told to guard our reputations obsessively. Jesus certainly wasn't too concerned about his. We're much more worried about our image than about our actual thoughts and behavior, and that's wrong.

*A spiritually mature person is always in control of his or her passions.* That may be true, but it isn't observable. Jesus looked pretty out of control when he erupted in public by calling the teachers of the law hypocrites, sons of hell, snakes, blind guides, and whitewashed tombs that looked clean on the outside but were full of stinking, decaying bodies on the inside.[6] He also looked out of control when he was overcome with anger in the Temple court and began turning over the tables, recklessly scattering money everywhere, and slashing at people and livestock with a spur-of-the-moment whip. He was, according to his disciples, consumed with zeal.[7]

Outbursts of anger and fits of rage are on Paul's lists of what a sinful nature looks like,[8] so we know these things can appear evil. And in many cases in our own lives, it's obvious that our anger is misplaced and inappropriately expressed. But our unwritten rule that true spirituality is always calm is not valid. That's what we *expect* Christian maturity to look like, not what the Bible says it is.

The truth is that spiritual maturity involves having the right passions about the right things at the right times and expressing them in the right ways. Sometimes our passions can be as demonstrative as Jesus' were, and it doesn't mean we're out of control or sinning. In fact, I believe it's worse to be passive in areas where God is outraged than to be over-expressive about things that concern him. None of us actually witnessed Jesus in his physical body when he came, but I'm pretty sure he didn't walk around with a vacant stare speaking in a calm, wispy voice like he does in many of the Jesus movies. The Gospels indicate some pretty passionate responses of grief and anger—"loud crying and tears," says one New Testament writer[9]—and he was perceived by members of his own family and residents of his hometown as being a regular guy.[10] He was and is as spiritually mature as someone can get, yet zealous and passionate in his expressions.

*Boasting is clear evidence of pride.* Imagine going to a conference and hearing the speaker say the following. "I'm the only chance you have of knowing God."[11] "You know your city's greatest piece of architecture—that massive piece of pride and joy where God meets with you? Knock it down, and I'll build it better in three days."[12] "If you think God giving you bread out of heaven is something, wait till you discover who *I* am."[13] "God and I are one and the same."[14] "If you believe in me, you'll live forever."[15]

How would you respond to such claims? Nearly everyone I know, myself included, would become practically nauseated by the pride oozing from such statements. Even if that speaker did some miracles and said some extremely profound things, most of us would say he's a slick salesman or a satanic deceiver. And those charges are, in fact, some of the responses Jesus received from most of the educated people of his day. The people who were impressed by his claims were, for the most part, the kind of people our bloggers would call "gullible" and "ignorant of Scripture." When we read the Gospels today, we call them "people of great faith."

*Spiritual maturity involves having the right passions about the right things at the right times and expressing them in the right ways.*

Jesus didn't boast; he told the truth. But the truth sounded awfully proud.[16] He claimed a special relationship with God that no one else had (though he welcomed others into that relationship). He claimed to be the key to life (and invited anyone who wanted to experience true life to accept his love). He claimed that all sacred Scripture for the last 1,500 years was really about him (including the parts about his extreme suffering and sacrificial love). And he claimed to have conquered evil and death (and offered us the spoils of his war). If our internal alarms had gone off with the first part of each of those sentences—the parts not in parentheses—our outrage over his arrogance might have caused us to miss the Son of God. If we had been open enough to wait for the proof he offered, we'd have had eternal life.

*Being at the center of frequent controversy is a sign that something's wrong.* How do you feel about newsmakers who always seem to be at the center of some sort of ruckus—opinionated and divisive comments, allegations of wrongdoing, and the like? If you're like most people, you tire of the attention these people get and eventually just want them to fade into oblivion. There's something annoying about overexposure in TV headlines and tabloid covers. The media loves controversial figures. Nearly everyone else is bothered by them.

Narrow that example down a little further and ask yourself how you feel about *Christians* who are frequently in the middle of controversy. Isn't our assumption that where there's smoke, there's fire? Except with Jesus, there was always lots of smoke. (There was fire too, but not the negative kind.) Yet the controversy, the smoke, and the disruption in people's lives were part and parcel of his mission. They were ordained by God himself. But I'm not sure many evangelicals would even be open to the historical Jesus in their midst.

If Jesus were a member of one of our small-group Bible studies, I think there would come a time when we—in his own best interests, of course—would feel it necessary to organize an intervention and say something like: "Let's step back and take a look at the situation, Jesus. People are calling you a drunkard and accusing you of getting up close and personal with prostitutes. And not just once; this has become a pattern for you. But then when you're confronted on it, you somehow think all the people who talk about you are the ones with the problem?

"Listen, blaming people is basically a refusal to take responsibility for your own decisions. I mean, think about it: the one common denominator in all these conflicts is *you*. That should tell you something right there. Either all of these other people are uniformly wrong, or you are.

Now which seems more likely? Doesn't it seem a little more rational for you to face the problem by looking in the mirror? It's okay to admit flaws. We all have them. We'll walk you through whatever problem you're having. We're here for you, Jesus."

Sounds sort of blasphemous, doesn't it? Yet many of us who have been steeped in principles of discipleship for years might really have a problem with some of Jesus' behavior and attitudes. We'd see a lot of red flags in the things he did and said, and we'd want to rein him in. In fact, I believe that even if we were convinced that some of his miracles were valid, we'd still want to put some boundaries around his ministry and try to help him refine his theology a little bit.

I believe that's because of the emphasis we place on practical wisdom—in itself, a very good thing. But there's a difference between a "Proverbs Christian" and a "Gospels Christian." Proverbs is a collection of biblical wisdom that describes the principles of normal life, the ground rules for how to live in a godly way in the midst of a world with lots of distractions and temptations. If you want to live your life based purely on a set of principles, Proverbs is a great place to get them. They are divinely inspired instructions that set the standard for falling in line with the rhythms of the world as God designed them to function.

The problem is that Jesus didn't necessarily live according to Proverbs. He didn't have any counselors advising him of the wisdom of going to the cross. He bypassed that rule about a kind word turning away wrath, and it got him killed. And he somehow missed out on that promise about one's enemies being at peace with him when his ways are pleasing to the Lord.[17] God thundered from heaven that he was well pleased with his Son, yet his Son's enemies were certainly not at peace with him. Why?

How can we reconcile this apparent discrepancy between inspired Scripture and God incarnate? Only by realizing that radical faith and obedience often compel us to live independently of normal expectations and to see beyond the principles that usually rule us. We can't deny the wisdom of Proverbs and say that it's only good advice; it's much more than that. It's inspired Scripture—all true, but subject to greater truths that take precedence.

For example, quite a few proverbs emphasize advance planning and cautiousness and diligence, yet Jesus comes along and tells us to take no thought for our lives and to lay up our treasures in heaven rather than on earth. That isn't a contradiction in facts, but it's certainly a different emphasis—and a deeper, greater truth than that found in the wisdom of Solomon. Or, for an example outside of Proverbs, the law of Moses says, "You must purge the evil from among you. . . . Show no pity: life for life, eye for eye, tooth for tooth, hand for hand, foot for foot" (Deuteronomy 19:19, 21, NIV). That's certainly a true picture of justice, but there's a greater truth in the Kingdom of God: "But I tell you, Do not resist an evil person. If someone strikes you on the right cheek, turn to him the other also. And if someone wants to sue you and take your tunic, let him have your cloak as well" (Matthew 5:39-40, NIV).

So we can get great insight from divine legalities and Proverbs-style wisdom, but we can't confine ourselves to them and say anything else is contrary to God's Word. No, in a fallen world, principles for wise living often have to be submitted to the radical call of God to break out of the status quo. That's what Jesus did. And he called us to follow him and be remade in his non-status-quo image.

> *Principles for wise living often have to be submitted to the radical call of God to break out of the status quo. That's what Jesus did.*

I'm not recommending that we all start living more recklessly, preferring bad company to good, hinting at inappropriate relationships, bragging about our position in Christ, or stirring up controversy just so we can say we're spiritual. I do, however, think we need to stop making assumptions of people who, in our eyes, do these things. The life of Jesus teaches us emphatically that not all that appears to be inappropriate, prideful, contentious, or questionable actually is. We still need to hate sin, but we aren't supposed to hate everything that looks like it might be sin when we look at it through skeptical lenses and interpret it in the most damaging way. Relationships have been destroyed by such assumptions.

Whenever you see a believer in suspicious circumstances, ask yourself first if, to your knowledge, that person has actually sinned. Not if you think it looks probable that he or she sinned or violated one of the fences you've erected around the gospel, but if you actually know that he or she sinned. If not, withhold judgment. If you have a responsibility to hold that person accountable, then inquire about it in a spirit of "just checking." But there's no need to spread discord by raising your eyebrows in the presence of others, either literally or figuratively. That's how people reacted to Jesus, and they were very, very wrong.

## FORGOTTEN MESSAGES FROM JESUS:

+ Controversy can be ordained by God. "Smooth" and "status quo" are not always signs of his presence.
+ If it hints at immorality, smells like immorality, and even looks like immorality, it still might not be immoral. It could be bold and risky faith.
+ What appears as pride might simply be a humble declaration of the truth.
+ What appears as out-of-control passion might actually be Spirit-controlled passion.
+ There are many sides to biblical wisdom, and sometimes godly principles are overshadowed by greater truths. But only in the context of intimate fellowship with God can we know when this is so. A person saturated in the Spirit might be prompted to deviate from a strict biblical principle.[18]

# THAT SMELLS FISHY

PEOPLE ARE MESSY. All people—even God's chosen, redeemed sons and daughters. We'd like to think there's a stage of maturity and purity where our spiritual life flows freely and smoothly, even admirably, with the favor of God on our lives obvious to all observers. But God's favor is a tricky thing. It's tangible to those who have it and to many with sensitive spiritual eyes, but it looks very suspicious to others. It doesn't always come with the hallmarks of success; it isn't bestowed exclusively on radically pure hearts; and it's frequently accompanied by plenty of opposition. In other words, God's favor is poured out on messy lives, and it doesn't always clean up every mess. In fact, it can make certain aspects of life much messier.

It should be profoundly comforting that the heroes of Scripture were perceived as weird, flawed, incompetent, foolish, and even less than pure. That makes any of us eminently qualified to fulfill God's purposes. The amazing thing about their lives was what God did in them, not what they did themselves. Sometimes humility, honesty, and desperate faith were all they had to offer, but those are priceless commodities in the economy of God. We don't treasure them as much as he does, but we should. He has proven again and again that he wants us to come to him on those very simple but uncomfortable terms. Even when other people think there's something fishy about us.

+ + + +

# CHAPTER 11

# ROGUE EVANGELISM

The staff meeting continued late into the evening. It always did. For a church this size, getting through an agenda in less than three hours was virtually impossible. Usually it was more like five. Sometimes the items at the end of the list, when everyone wanted to go home, were approved with minimal discussion. Not this time.

"Okay, let's take a look at the last item on the agenda," said Mike, the executive pastor. "As you can see here, we're thinking of hosting this evangelist who needs a church to serve as his ministry base while he's in town. Temporarily, of course, and at no cost to us. He just needs some office space to call headquarters and a congregation to call home. So we'd be tied to him in name but not on paper. It will help with his credibility. Has anyone had a chance to look at his proposal yet?"

"Yeah, I've skimmed it," Brian volunteered. "He's had a lot of good results wherever he's been. Could be an asset here. Let's go for it."

"Whoa, slow down. Have you actually read his testimony? Or his references?" Lenny's cautious approach was often appreciated, but rarely at this hour. Not that anyone so thick-skinned and gruff really cared. He'd take all night if he had to.

"Lenny, come on." Brian rolled his eyes. "It won't cost us a thing, and he's been really effective at bringing people in. He'd be great for outreach—which you've always said we need more of, by the way."

"We do, but we've gotta know what we're getting into. Where does he stand on our doctrine? Has he caused any friction at other churches where he's been? Do we actually know any of his references? Or is he just breezing into town to sell whatever he's teaching and then leaving us to disciple his converts once he's gone? Listen, we've earned a pretty good reputation over the years. I don't want some circuit rider undoing it."

Phyllis cleared her throat. "Um, I've been reading his résumé while you've been talking. One thing that concerns me—it's hard to tell how long he'd stay. Some places he stays a couple of weeks, sometimes a couple of months, sometimes a couple of years. I don't think we want to host him forever, do we? Has he said what his plans are?"

"No," Mike said. "I think he stays until he feels like it's time to go, and then he says God's leading him somewhere else."

Lenny laughed. "Well, that's pretty suspicious. Fleece the flock and then get out of town."

"It does seem like a strange way to operate a ministry, Mike," said Phyllis. "If he's in the habit of running as soon as the going gets tough, I'm not sure we want to be left with that. Is that your impression?"

"No, I don't think he runs away from a situation. He's stuck it out through some pretty hard circumstances."

"Yeah, he'll sacrifice himself for Jesus as long as people are still buying what he's selling," Lenny muttered.

"Wow, Lenny, how'd you get to be so cynical?" Brian said, clearly resenting the fact that a real discussion was developing. "Have you considered that maybe he's actually sensitive to the Spirit?"

As usual, Brian and Lenny were on opposite sides of the fence. And, as usual, Phyllis tried to bridge the gap between them. "Well, I don't get the impression from his references and his reputation that he's running a scam, Lenny. Although, from what his references say here, he's apparently not at all shy about asking congregations for money. Still, there's no need to rush to judgment. But I do think it's fair to question how thorough he is in following up with people. It seems like he's restless. Gets discontented quickly and can't sit still. He doesn't have any roots, to speak of. Not a great example to have around in light of Pastor's recent sermons about consumer Christianity and church-hopping. Maybe this guy has a problem getting close to people, so he leaves as soon as that starts to happen. Or maybe it's worse than that . . . he does seem to have a tendency to create controversy."

"That's the last thing we need," Lenny stressed. "The *last* thing."

Listening carefully to everyone's opinions, Bob finally chimed in. "Um, guys, have any of you read this testimony?"

"Not yet," Mike admitted. "I heard he has a pretty shady past but also a dramatic conversion experience. That was several years ago, though."

"Well, I think this is a little more serious than a shady past."

"I'm sure whatever it is," Brian sighed, "God has enough grace to cover it."

Phyllis wanted to hear more. "What do you mean, Bob?"

"Um, if I'm reading this right . . . he used to, um, get rid of Christians."

"Get rid of? What does *that* mean?"

"Like, kill them. Or try to get them arrested. He hated us, apparently."

"Oh, come on," Lenny scoffed. "That's a little much. I've heard of exaggerating a testimony for dramatic effect, but that's just way over the top. He's a con artist, people."

"I think he's serious, Lenny. He's got some pretty specific details in here. And he certainly isn't bragging about it."

"You know," Phyllis said, her face turning pale as she looked up from the papers, "this really wasn't very long ago. I might feel more comfortable with him being here if it had been twenty years, but this is much more recent. That's a little unsettling to me."

"Well, that makes it even more obvious he's lying," Lenny growled. "How's he explaining killing people a few years ago and not doing any time for it? That just isn't possible. You wouldn't write about a felony that you could still get arrested for."

"No, it was overseas somewhere," Bob said. "I guess in a country that tolerates that sort of thing—if it's against Christians, I mean."

"Yeah, somewhere where they don't speak English and it's impossible to verify what he's saying. Like I said, con artist."

"Regardless of the fact that our members probably won't ever be comfortable with someone like this, I think it's really important in the community for a minister to have a spotless reputation," Phyllis said. "When this much controversy follows somebody, something's wrong. I don't think we want to be associated with a ministry like that."

"Well, I have to agree that this changes everything," Brian admitted. "I don't know if his testimony is true or not, but I look at it like this: If it isn't true, like Lenny thinks—exaggerated, lying, whatever—it's a huge character flaw. And if it is, then he's an unconvicted murderer. Either way, he shouldn't be coming here. We don't need cameras from *America's Most Wanted* outside our church to show the last place he's been. The decent thing to do would be for him to withdraw from ministry. But really he should turn himself in."

"Actually," said Bob, "it looks like he's already been in prison. Oh, wait . . . not for murder, though. It was since then . . . since he's been a Christian. Causing a riot overseas, apparently."

Lenny looked around the room, astonished. "So can anybody tell me why in the world we're still talking about this?"

"Yeah, good point," Mike said. "Even on the slim chance he's on the up-and-up, it's too risky. Too much potential for disaster. Anybody still in favor? . . . Okay, then, I'll let him know tomorrow. Meeting adjourned. Go home and get some rest."

+ + + +

Evangelical Christians idealize Paul, and that's understandable. After all, he worked tirelessly and sacrificially under extreme circumstances to preach the gospel and build churches in cities across the empire. His perseverance, passion, insight, and willingness to lay down his life are inspiring. His ability to understand, interpret, and teach Christian truth is amazing. His explanations of the doctrine of justification by grace through faith have become pillars of the church for nearly two millennia. Because of the unique calling on his life and the vast influence God allowed him to have even in his own time, his letters became foundational documents for the early church. His evangelistic, discipleship, and leadership methods became templates for the global spread of the gospel. More than a quarter of our New Testament was written by him.

All of the attention we give to Paul makes him one of the most popular figures in church history. But if Paul were making the rounds in our churches today, we'd have quite a few complaints about him. Many Christians who celebrate his ministry in retrospect would have rejected it at the time. Paul would not be very popular in contemporary American Christianity.

Why would we react negatively to

> *Many Christians who celebrate Paul's ministry in retrospect would have rejected it at the time.*

such a giant of the faith? Well, imagine our response to a minister today who frequently asked for money, wrote angry and forceful letters to his constituents, created controversy wherever he went, exerted a high level of authority over the church in general, had public run-ins with other church leaders, claimed to have visited heaven in indescribable mystical experiences, had been beaten by mobs on numerous occasions, and had been in and out of prison more than a few times. Not only that, some of his practices and beliefs were more than a little controversial—like speaking directly to evil spirits and letting handkerchiefs that had touched him be used to heal the sick.[1] Is that the kind of minister you'd host in your church? Probably not.

All of those incidents, of course, occurred after Paul became a Christian. His pre-Christian experience included spearheading a rather bloody inquisition against messianic Jews.[2] If he had been a drug addict or a celebrity hedonist and then got saved, our churches would love him. But the leader of a murderous genocide against Christians? an operative for state-sponsored terrorism? It would take a lot of mercy to overlook such a heinous past and embrace a minister with crimes against humanity on his record. Most churches in our culture wouldn't be able to do it.

It isn't just the modern church that would have a problem with Paul. Many of the Christians of his own day did too. Though some churches followed him eagerly,[3] others questioned his motives, his visions, his authority, his temperament, his doctrine, and his methods.[4] Some seemed to view his hardships, his penchant for controversy, and his numerous critics as signs that he wasn't in the will of God.[5] Rival ministers viewed him as competition and preached Christ out of envy.[6] False teachers contradicted his teachings and undermined his ministry.[7] He was loved by many and resented by many more.

In today's Christian culture, we'd give Paul some stellar advice about his methodology: "It seems like every time you start to get close to people, you move again.[8] No wonder you can't even remember who you've baptized. Seems like you've bought into consumer Christianity, Paul. Always shopping for the right church. You have to invest yourself in one place for a longer period of time; otherwise, you'll never really get a ministry going before you pick up and leave again. Furthermore, Paul, you have to find the right balance between asking for money and trying to earn it all yourself. It's okay to receive a modest salary, so you don't have to work your fingers to the bone every night. On the other hand, you won't stop talking about how much money you need for famine relief in Judea. It gives the wrong impression, like you're preaching for entertainment and then asking for an offering instead of applause. I realize it's a worthy cause, but too much talk about sacrificial giving just turns people off."

We would also offer him some choice counsel about his teaching style: "You're way too intense, and it turns people off. You plead with them while tears are running down your face like you've known them for twenty years, you go back and forth between being gentle and forceful, you use extremely long run-on sentences, and your personality always seems to divide people and create controversy. And speaking of 'way too often,' can you stop telling the same testimony over and over again? I think it's pretty well known by now. You act like that's the biggest thing that ever happened to you."[9]

About his teaching itself: "How can you justify blasting Peter for eating kosher and then turn around and insist on getting Timothy circumcised?[10] Who's compromising with whom? Don't you think that's just a tad hypocritical? And then you get really harsh and call people dogs and evildoers simply for practicing the same things they've always been taught to practice. It's not like Jewish habits are sinful. Can't you just deal with their points without mudslinging? Oh, and that business about all of us being 'dead' and 'children of wrath': too dramatic, too insensitive, too negative. You need to tone it down a bit. And quit using all that legal Pharispeak that you and your boarding-school buddies grew up on. You're great at making really forceful points about theological technicalities that people don't actually care to know."

And about his lifestyle: "How many times do you have to get thrown in jail before you change careers? Is this really what God wants you to do with your life—stir people up until all they want to do is throw rocks at you? Do you think those officials enjoy beating people? They're just trying to keep the peace in their city, and you're like public enemy number one on that count. Find a place to settle down and stop all this constant traveling. It isn't a balanced way to live—or to earn an income, for that matter. You're basically working for tips that churches will give you. And the number of churches that like you enough for that is getting smaller, in case you haven't noticed."

Paul would suffer today from a social dynamic we hardly notice among ourselves. As a ministry increases in influence, its critics multiply exponentially. The growth ratio of supporters to attackers is horribly disproportionate in favor of the attackers. It seems that the more people benefit from a particular ministry, the greater our need to point out how those people are being misled. It has happened again and again. A ministry functions without any backlash because it's doctrinally sound and changing lives. But if its message gets enough attention to have the look and feel of a trend, critics will go searching for nitpicky details to undermine it. Maybe they assume that only a watered-down gospel can have popular appeal, or perhaps they're trying to justify why their ministries aren't doing well in spite of their faithfulness. Regardless, they'll turn doctrinal molehills into mountains of "danger" so they can cut mountains of ministry back down to molehills of effectiveness. If that's not competition and jealousy within the body of Christ, I don't know what is.

> *As a ministry increases in influence, its critics multiply exponentially.*

Paul seemed to wear a target on his back sometimes, and not all the attacks came from non-Christian opponents. Some preached out of jealousy and strife while he was in prison, capitalizing on his groundwork in order to make a name for themselves. No matter, he wrote; at least Christ was being preached.[11]

And don't think Paul wouldn't wear that same target today. If he were an enigma of the present rather than a hero of the past, I suspect that discerning Christians would be explaining all the ways he diverges from historical, orthodox Christianity. Never mind that he profoundly shaped our definition of historical, orthodox Christianity in the first place. The critics would find something. They always do. They'd pick a statement out of context that could be taken the wrong way, and then assume that the speaker meant it the wrong way. Next thing you know, the speaker gets blasted for something he never really intended to say. It's a straw-man extravaganza. No wonder Paul said to beware of the dogs.[12]

Our tendency to overemphasize secondary issues might also lead us to blast Paul's ministry. I'm not particularly interested in a more generous orthodoxy in the sense that some are,[13] but I do believe we need to loosen up a little on issues that aren't spelled out exactly for us in the Bible. (First we need to admit that some of our pet interpretations of *the* biblical perspective on those issues aren't all that convincing.) Doctrine aside, however, I'm certainly in favor of a more generous methodology. I don't think Paul's personality, practices, leadership style, theological arguments, and ministry relationships would be quite so admired today because we impose our Christian culture so forcefully on many of our denominations and institutions. There are unstated rules for Christian society, especially in leadership circles, that have nothing to do with biblical norms. And some of our chapter-and-verse support for those rules is strained, at best. But we love having those standards around. They're like a secret handshake only the insiders know.

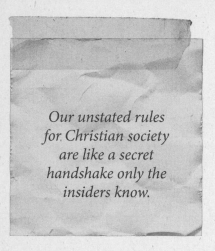

*Our unstated rules for Christian society are like a secret handshake only the insiders know.*

For example, I've heard ministries criticized for worship that's too informal (or too formal), for not having a pulpit (or only having a movable pulpit); for using the wrong translation of the Bible; for being too seeker friendly or not seeker friendly enough; for preaching a message that's too positive or too negative; for having support groups for people dealing with divorce, substance abuse, or sexual addictions; and more. In other eras, churches were condemned for having Sunday school (a British import), having racially mixed congregations, or allowing women to serve in leadership positions of any kind. Some of these issues are more significant than others, but none are directly addressed in the Bible. Over the course of history, we've come up with all kinds of biblical arguments for each side of these issues, but none of them fall into the category of scriptural absolutes. We've simply had a remarkable ability to make phantom doctrine out of patchwork assumptions.

On a minor scale, there are aspects of our microcultures within the church that become much more rigid than they should. I've been in evangelical communities in which creative, free-spirit personalities were considered spiritually immature or undiscipled—or worse, "liberal"; in which not participating in a certain boycott was seen as a failure to do a Christian duty; and in which things like interracial marriage or even a large age difference in marriage was a scandal of biblical proportions. In some Christian circles, talking about being depressed or dealing with a family conflict is taken as evidence of not being close to God.

What comes to mind when I mention the word *evangelist*? How about *pastor*? or *prophet*? Most of us have a certain visual image that goes along with those words, and that image often comes from some extra-biblical assumptions. I remember one man's response when I told him I was applying to seminary; it was amusing to me but not altogether surprising. "But . . . you're kind of introverted," he said with a look of utter confusion on his face. I had to explain that a lot of people go to seminary to be something other than a pastor, and even if they didn't, there are plenty of pastors who aren't loud, slap-you-on-the-back extroverts. But that was a foreign concept to him, and it didn't make any sense. He acted as if I were violating some clear instruction in the pastoral epistles. I wasn't typical minister material.

I have to confess some strange feelings about a nonbiblical issue too. When I first started attending a church that meets on Saturday night, it seemed almost heretical to sleep in on Sunday morning. (I got over it pretty quickly.) The Sunday morning worship schedule had been a part of my life as long as I could remember. Now I was eating brunch among "the unchurched"—or among people who had been to worship services some other time during the week, just as I had. I discovered that God doesn't strike someone with lightning for violating extrabiblical traditions.

We often read the book of Acts and Paul's letters as definitive patterns for ministry, even though they don't make such claims for themselves.[14] But I don't think the methods of ministry in Acts and the Epistles define patterns for us as much as they set a precedent. And that precedent is that the ministry of the Holy Spirit is varied, creative, unpredictable, and dynamic. Anyone who tries to bottle the Spirit's methodology will grow frustrated (and fruitless) pretty quickly. Even Paul varied his methodology from place to place. *That's* our example. Endless variations on one absolute theme.

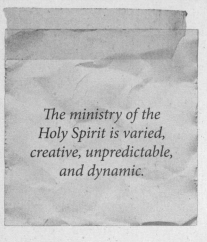

*The ministry of the Holy Spirit is varied, creative, unpredictable, and dynamic.*

Paul caught a lot of flak for his beliefs and methods, especially because the early church was still feeling its way through uncharted territory in both faith and practice. We benefit from their lack of precision in those years because they show us what it's like to follow the Spirit when you don't have a five-year strategic plan or even a New Testament to study. If we're honest with ourselves, we'll realize that our experience with highly developed ministries would have compelled us to advise Paul against many of his words and behaviors. This apostle, hand selected by God for one of history's greatest missions, wouldn't fit into many of our strategies today. Our high standards would have shut out the messy but powerful ministry of God's Spirit through Paul.

## FORGOTTEN MESSAGES FROM PAUL:

+ God's servants don't always have a stable employment history on their résumé.
+ Though God's Word never advocates situational ethics, it certainly endorses situational methods.
+ Christian leadership is not a popularity contest.
+ Sitting in prison is no indication in itself of being outside of God's will. Neither are controversies, shipwrecks, beatings, stonings, and public protests. It's entirely possible to be a Spirit-inspired troublemaker.

# CHAPTER 12

# IMMATURE PRAISE

**MODERATOR:** Welcome to the opening session of this year's convention of the National Organization for Worship Music and Expression. We're starting off with a panel discussion on writing original songs that glorify God. I'd like to welcome our panel . . . you may recognize some of the faces up here. On the far left, we have Ben Mishkan, one of the premier experts on Israel's worship during the time of David and Solomon; next to him is Beth Kinnor, a songwriter whose works have been sung by many of today's top Christian artists; then Dan Levitt, whom you'll recognize as the worship leader at the largest church in North America; and finally, on the right, Otto Givins, marketing expert and independent talent scout for several major record labels. I'll moderate the questions, and anyone who has one can step up to one of the microphones in the aisle. I'll call on you at the proper time, okay? I think our panel's ready, so let's get started. Microphone one, you're up. Please give us your name and where you're from before you ask your question.

**MAC:** Hi, my name is Mac, and I'm from Houston. It seems that there's a fine line between an atmosphere of real worship and a pep rally. My question is, how can we write songs that create a joyful mood without people getting too self-indulgent?

**BETH:** Great question, Mac. My initial reaction is that I'm not sure you really can. I mean, you're not responsible for the attitude of people's hearts when they're singing and, depending on what kind of church you're in, dancing. Whether it's genuine worship or self-centered recreation is really between that individual and God. That said, however, I think there are some things you can do to help people get past themselves and focus on God. And one thing is to write songs that center on God rather than on people.

**DAN**: I'd agree with that and add that the songs that focus on God need to focus on who he is rather than what he has done for us. When the words and music are all about him, it gives people less opportunity to obsess about their needs and desires. It turns people upward rather than inward.

**BEN**: That's a good point, Dan. And I think you'll find that this is what Hebrew worship was like during the time of David's Tabernacle and Solomon's Temple. Very focused on the attributes of God.

**OTTO**: I want to go back to another point the question raised. I'm not sure I see anything wrong with people having a great time while they worship.

**BEN**: Right, of course not. But there's a fine line between having a self-centered good time and rejoicing in the Lord. And I think we'd all acknowledge that this line gets crossed very often in many churches and gatherings. The worship musicians in Jerusalem during the first Temple era were always very reverent and divinely focused. And I think that's what we want to model.

**MODERATOR**: Okay, let's go on to the next question. Microphone number two, you're up.

**DAWN**: My name is Dawn, and I'm from Los Angeles. I wanted to follow up on something that was said by, I think, Dan. You mentioned that the words and music need to be about who God is rather than what he does for us. Could you elaborate on that a little? Like, what Scriptures would be good examples of this?

**DAN**: Well, Scripture in general is a good example—the whole Bible. The focus isn't on people's needs and desires and the favors God does, but on his holiness and majesty and wisdom and love. And I think in particular—and Ben can tell you more about this since he's the expert—the Psalms are a great place to go for examples of God-focused worship.

**BEN**: That's right, Dan. In fact, we can just open up right now and find a couple of examples. Can someone hand me a Bible?

**OTTO**: While you're doing that, Ben, let me just add that the music industry has often sold God to consumers as a kind of heavenly vending machine, and I think we're realizing that and moving past it to a deeper kind of worship. I know the labels I work with are interested in that, because frankly people are tired of me-centered spirituality.

**BETH**: That's true. If you look at the most popular songs over the last few years, you'll see a bit of a swing from the give-me-what-I-need lyrics, which really aren't worship, to now more of the praise-you-for-who-you-are lyrics. That's what I try to do in my songs, of course, and I sense a real desire among worship leaders like you to get past the "me" stage of spiritual growth, like my songs do.

**BEN**: All right, I've got my Bible open now. Let's take a look at a couple of choral psalms—as opposed to poetry or wisdom psalms—to start with. And I'm speaking specifically of those that have musical instructions at the top. Um . . . the first one we come to is Psalm 4. "Answer me when I call, O God of my righteousness! You have relieved me in my distress; be gracious to me and hear my . . ." Well, this is actually a prayer for help and safety, so maybe not the best one to start with. Let's see . . . well, actually, so is Psalm 5. Let me skip a little farther on. Look at Psalm 8, for example: "How majestic is Your name in all the earth." See, that's about God's attributes, not about what he does for us. And if you keep reading: You "have established strength because of Your adversaries, to make the enemy and the revengeful to cease. . . ." Well, it goes on to talk about how God has crowned human beings with majesty and glory, so a little of that "me" focus creeps into that one too. As you can tell, I didn't prepare for this . . . let me dig farther down . . . Psalm 21, for example: "In Your strength the king will be glad." See how David rejoices not in God's blessings but in God himself? And then . . . oh, wait. In this one David also talks about how God puts a crown of gold on his head and will give him long life, so again, not a pure example of the Bible's main emphasis. It shouldn't be hard to find a good model, though, because they're everywhere . . . I'll skip way ahead to get into the real meat of worship, like how Psalm 103 starts out—a classic example: "Bless the LORD, O my soul, and all that is within me, bless His holy name." Now that's a very pure form of worship, very God-centered. And I think that's what our worship today needs to sound like.

**MODERATOR**: Good. Let's move on to . . .

**DAWN:** Wait, can I follow that up real quick?

**MODERATOR:** Very quickly.

**DAWN:** Just to clarify . . . Psalm 103, which you just read from, goes right into God's benefits: He pardons iniquity, heals diseases, rescues us from the pit, satisfies us, and renews our youth. I mean, David is blessing the Lord because of these things. He even says to remember these things. So are you saying it's not okay to bring that kind of stuff into our worship?

**BEN:** Well, I think the point is that we need to seek God for God's sake, not worship him for what he does. And I think we all agree that this is the biblical model, even if those particular psalms I picked out, without any preparation time on my part, happened to mention a few of the things God has done. The overall emphasis in the Bible is on praising God for who he is, not for the gifts he gives.

**MODERATOR:** Very good. Next question, back to microphone one . . .

+ + + +

It sounds so noble, doesn't it? So much more spiritual and selfless than praising God for his favors. That would be understandable for the spiritually immature, kind of like a child who's more interested in the gift Daddy brings back from a business trip than spending time with Daddy himself. But as we grow, we move beyond that. Right?

Maybe *we* do, but no one in the Bible seemed to. David certainly didn't. Sure, he praised God with some of the most beautiful psalmody ever crafted, and much of it focused on God's attributes. But it rarely did so apart from recalling God's past gifts or hoping for his future blessings. His attributes are completely unknown apart from what he has done and what he has promised.

> *We can't know God unless we see what he's done and hear his voice.*

That's why nearly every psalm refers to an act of blessing or benefit of knowing and trusting God. In the same way that we can't know a person unless we witness that person's behavior, expressions, and words, we can't know God unless we see what he's done and hear his voice. And in Scripture, his works and his voice always come in the context of his actions—especially his blessings—toward his people.

If David were a worship musician in one of our churches today, I suspect he'd hear a mild chastisement from his lead pastors: "Dave, you have to get to a point in your walk with God where you're able to worship him just for who he is, not for what he gives you. Almost everything you've written says, 'I praise you because . . .' and then names something he's done for you—or that you *want* him to do for you. That's worshiping Santa Claus, David, not God."

I realize that the desire to worship God for his wonderful attributes

> *God has chosen to reveal himself—not in systematic theology or theory, but in real, raw, face-to-face encounters with his love, mercy, power, wisdom, and judgment.*

and character is good and pure and beautiful. To some extent, it truly is a sign of maturity. It's just unrealistic. And unnecessary. And, on top of that, impossible. We don't know anything about his attributes and character apart from the actual experiences of people in the Bible and, if we're in fellowship with him today, our own true-life experiences. That's how God has chosen to reveal himself—not in systematic theology or theory, but in real, raw, face-to-face encounters with his love, mercy, power, wisdom, and even judgment. God demonstrates who he is and what he's like in life, in the stories of real people in history, and in our subjective observation of his subjective personality. That's the God of the Bible.

Our emphasis on God's glory comes about for a very good reason. Evangelicalism has produced a self-centered strain of faith that constantly asks, "What can God do for me?" From that perspective, prayers become a shopping list—and the desire to actually know God for who he is falls to the very bottom of the list. In order to correct that imbalance, we're now stressing that "it's all about him, not about me." This emphasis is understandable—it encourages people to look beyond what's going on in their immediate lives. In principle, that's a noble effort. In practice, it's unworkable—and a contradiction of what God actually says in his Word.

The problem is that the gospel's centerpiece is God's sacrificial love, and without an object of that love at the center of the centerpiece, the sacrifice really doesn't mean very much. For a sacrifice to have meaning, it has to have a purpose, an object valued enough to sacrifice for. That points us right back to ourselves, the objects of God's affection. He wants our lives to revolve around him rather than around ourselves, of course; we're being made in his image, so we need to have sacrificial love for a purpose too. But he never means for us to take ourselves out of the picture. His love is lavished on us for us to enjoy and appreciate. For that to happen, we have to be in the picture.

Think about it like this: An artist's masterpiece certainly shows us something about the artist himself, and most people who admire the art also admire the artist. But they never really get to a stage of ignoring the masterpiece in order to focus on the master (unless, of course, they're working on a doctoral thesis or have been assigned by the news desk to do a feature story on the artist—in which case, people will read the information, say "hmmm, that's interesting," and then turn their attention back to the art). It isn't that no one cares about the personality of the artist; but they care only because they have intriguing visual evidence of the artist's personality. And most artists, I would think, prefer it that way. They love to be appreciated for their work. After all, the work expresses who they are, and it's the work that they put before the public. There's great satisfaction in doing something well and being commended for it.

God makes it clear in Scripture that he loves being commended for the excellence of his work. He's like an artist who's always having to remind his people to look at his craftsmanship. He says, "Did you see what I did for you? What do you think of my love and my ability? Tell me about it!" After the Exodus, he very frequently instructed Israel to remember him as the one who rescued them out of Egypt. When he revealed himself to Moses, who was hidden in the cleft of a rock, he identified his attributes as they apply to human beings—compassionate, gracious, slow to anger, forgiving our sins, and blessing our generations.[1]

Isaiah instructs us to "praise the LORD in song, *for He has done excellent things*" (Isaiah 12:5, italics added). Paul begins Ephesians with a blessing to God, praising him for providing us with every spiritual blessing—and he goes on in the next eleven verses to list quite a few things that God has done *for us*.[2] So when we attempt to separate the gifts from the Giver, we're ignoring clear biblical precedent.

I understand the heart behind that, but when we're so zealous about not being "we-centered" that we make the gospel "we-irrelevant," we're undermining the very glory we're trying to defend. God's glory can't be separated from those in whom it is being revealed. In one sense, it's true that the gospel isn't "about us," but in another sense, it isn't the gospel without us. We're so intent on pointing out that the Bible is God-centered that we end up with a different standard than the Bible actually uses.

> *God's glory can't be separated from those in whom it is being revealed.*

For example, I recently heard a prominent member of the evangelical community on a Webcast criticizing a song popularized by Michael W. Smith. The last line of the song says, "Like a rose trampled on the ground, you took the fall and thought of me . . . above all."[3] No, said the critic, that's wrong. God didn't think of us above all. God's life doesn't revolve around our agenda. His primary motivation for the gospel was to display his glory, not to save us. The song is too me-centered, he said, and very theologically incorrect (the evangelical version of "politically incorrect").

The problem with this person's commentary was that it ignored the facts. The Bible repeatedly and emphatically refers to what Jesus did *for us*. Yes, the gospel demonstrates God's glory—that's beyond question. But the part of the gospel that glorifies God most is the astounding fact that the Creator of the universe would make such an enormous sacrifice for rebels like us. If Jesus died for his own glory alone, we're able to praise God in our theology. But if he died to save us out of a miserable condition and to meet our needs, then we praise him in the deepest places of our heart. And that, as numerous testimonies would indicate, is exactly the response many have had upon hearing songs that focus on his sacrifice on our behalf.

I'm sure God appreciates our selfless concern for his glory, but Scripture really does bring us into the equation quite a bit. "God demonstrates His own love *toward us*, in that while we were yet sinners, Christ died *for us*" (Romans 5:8, italics added). Paul writes: "With humility of mind regard one another as more important than yourselves" (Philippians 2:3) and goes on to say that Jesus is the prime example of that attitude. (In other words, he thought of us over himself.) That same passage stresses that Jesus considered his own life expendable for the sake of those he came to save. John said, "We know love by this, that He laid down His life *for us*" (1 John 3:16, italics added). And I don't think I've ever read a translation of John 3:16 that says, "For God so loved his own glory that he gave his only begotten Son . . ." No, he loved *us*. He died for *us*. He humbled himself on our behalf.

It sounds very selfless to take human beings out of the salvation story, but it's really kind of arrogant. More often than not, there's a certain smugness oozing out of it, a spiritual pride that seems to imply that the speaker has risen above immature, me-centered Christianity. It's like saying, "No, Lord, Scripture places way too much emphasis on us. You don't get enough glory the way you've worded it here. We need to stick up for you." And the Lord, I think, responds with a smile: "You don't understand me very well, do you? My humble sacrifice on your behalf *is* my glory."

> *The false dichotomy between God's glory and his benefits to us fails to take into account the fact that God is glorified by our responses to him.*

Now, are there verses that say that the gospel is in fact a demonstration of God's glory? Absolutely.[4] God's honor or renown is ultimately the highest value in the universe. But there's no reason for us to make a distinction between his benefits and our praise. God's gifts and his glory are intertwined. In a prayer in which he talked about his own glory a lot, Jesus made this remarkable statement to the Father: "The glory which You have given Me I have given to them, that they may be one, just as We are one" (John 17:22). How would you react if a Christian publicly said, "Jesus gave me his glory so he and I can be united as one person"? Unless someone in the audience were on the ball enough to remind everyone that Jesus expressed this very thought in his high-priestly prayer, the theology police would respond quickly and efficiently. "Self-centered and blasphemous," I think they'd call it, with a sharp reminder that "it's all about him, not about us"—forgetting, obviously, that the Cross put him and us on the same side of the fence. This isn't an either/or proposition. It's about him *and* about us.

This false dichotomy between God's glory and his benefits to us fails to take into account the fact that God is glorified by our responses to him. Obviously we are not meant to pursue a selfish, one-sided relationship with him; but the other extreme would be the kind of faith that selflessly ignores what he offers and promises us—which, in effect, amounts to rejecting his gifts. That doesn't glorify him at all. When God says, "Remember what I've done for you," and we fail to do that because we want to be completely God-centered, we're essentially being disobedient. In many respects, our role as human beings is to bask in the Father's love and experience his mercies. Not to abuse them, but simply to experience them. And to be very, very grateful for his blessings. To some degree, that involves seeking those blessings. That glorifies him, blending me-centered faith and God-centered faith into we-centered faith. He wants us to see ourselves as one with him. The "all of you, none of me" approach ignores that unity.

For that reason, our response to the common what-can-God-do-for-me theology is an overreaction. It's well intentioned, to be sure; and it does a good job of rebuking selfish faith, which is important. But correcting the imbalance of selfish faith with another imbalance is misguided. Our zeal for a God-centered/me-irrelevant Christianity takes the good news out of the Good News. If we applied our corrective theology to David or Paul the way we apply it to songwriters, speakers, and writers today, we'd be attacking huge portions of Scripture. We'd expose the fact that our biblical perspective isn't very biblical at all.

## FORGOTTEN MESSAGES FROM DAVID:

+ The Bible never pits the blessings God gives against the glory he receives. The two go hand in hand. It's fine to worship God for what he has done in your life.

+ When God-centered theology pushes the story of human redemption into the background of Scripture, it essentially detracts from the glory of God—the opposite of the intended effect.
+ A hypercritical, nitpicky dissection of someone else's worship dishonors God. Period. It's a private moment between that person and God. Any outside opinions are intruding.

# CHAPTER 13

# PRINCIPLES OF INEFFECTIVE LEADERSHIP

"What's with the sudden staff meeting, Grant?" Laura asked. "This isn't the most convenient time of the week, you know."

"Yeah, but I had to keep it kind of quiet. I think we have a serious matter to deal with, and the sooner the better."

Josh looked around the room and noticed the empty spot where the pastor usually sat. "Shouldn't we wait for Marcus?"

"Marcus isn't coming," Grant answered abruptly.

"Ooohhh." Celeste raised her eyebrows. "I've been wondering when this meeting was going to happen."

"Yeah, it's time. The board has been noisier than usual lately. Let's get it out on the table."

Josh frowned. "What are you talking about? Why isn't the pastor coming?"

"Because he's the problem, Josh."

"Wait a minute . . . this is a coup? How can you even consider replacing someone as godly as he is?"

"This is a church, Josh," Grant said with a forced smile. "We don't have 'coups.' But yes, we do need to consider the effectiveness of our ministry, and Marcus's job is on the line. We aren't making an impact in our community. We aren't growing. Giving is down. And it's been this way for nearly three years. We're headed in the wrong direction."

"I agree," said Celeste. "This is a stewardship issue. I know he hired all of us except Grant, and I know you're especially loyal to him, Josh. That's great. But this isn't about friendship or loyalty—or how godly he is. We're slipping fast, and his vision isn't even close to being realized. We need a fresh vision. New blood. And a strong leader."

"He *is* a strong leader," Josh pleaded. "Just because he's humble and unassuming doesn't mean he isn't strong."

"But he's been here five years, and the last three haven't been good," Laura countered.

"Depends on how you define 'good,'" Josh muttered. "Numbers aren't everything. Maybe God is preparing us for growth."

"That's what dying churches say to make themselves feel better." Grant's tone was growing sharper. He wasn't going to back down.

"Okay, but don't you remember that revival he was at the center of a few years before he came here? It was amazing. Miracles happening right and left. His last church was sputtering, too, but every time they got too low, God did something amazing. And it's because he's a man of prayer. He'd get the whole church on their knees repenting. They'd get a huge gift or an influx of new people or something out of the blue like that. As much as they worried, he never did. And they never had to shut their doors."

"Well, I don't remember all the details of his old church," Celeste said with a sigh, "and really, what does that matter? He came here with this big vision and it isn't happening. We're not going in the direction he promised us. I feel like we're in limbo, and in my mind, that's a waste of time. We could be growing stronger in a community like this—changing lives around us—but we're still trying to figure out how to stop going around in circles."

Josh put his face in his hands. "And you don't think we're making progress?"

"Have you seen our receipts this quarter?" Laura chuckled. "No, we're not making progress. When was the last time we filled the baptistery? How many new members classes have we held lately?"

"I agree," Grant said. "And it isn't like our city is stagnant. Have you seen all the houses going up? Our area is growing. But not the church. Something's wrong here. Under Marcus, we're stumbling aimlessly while the other churches around us are getting bigger."

"Well, I don't think we're stumbling, and I certainly don't think Marcus is aimless," Josh said. "I think God's doing a deep work in us, and we'll eventually see the fruit."

"I'm sorry, Josh," said Laura, "but I don't think the board is going to be that patient. Frankly, neither am I. I think we can do much better."

"Who do you suggest, Laura?" Celeste asked.

Grant shook his head. "That's a discussion for later. We'll do the usual—get together a committee, have a full-blown pastor search, pray for the right man, and—"

"Or woman." Celeste laughed. "No reason to think one of us couldn't be promoted, you know?"

"Well, it could be one of us. That's true," Grant agreed. "In fact, I think any one of us in this room would do a better job. Less talking and more walking. That's what we need."

Laura nodded. "So what's the next step?"

"I feel obligated to tell him what's up," Josh said.

Grant jerked his head suddenly and stared at Josh. "No, no, no, don't you dare," he said in his most intimidating voice. Josh had always thought that if churches were playgrounds, Grant would be the bully. In fact, he was starting to wonder if churches were more like playgrounds than he'd thought.

"Definitely not," Celeste added. "Now that we're in agreement—"

"But we're *not* in agreement!"

"Now that the majority has spoken, Josh," she continued, "we should call an official meeting to let the board know they have the staff's support. Or *most* of the staff's support. It's up to them to move forward, right, Grant?"

"Right. It's not our place to initiate any action. And honestly, if it makes you feel any better, Josh, they would have gone ahead with this even if we hadn't met. They don't actually need our agreement. But I'm sure they'll be glad they have it. It will make things easier if we can present a unified front to the congregation."

"Well, it will never be completely unified because I can't go along with this."

"That's our Josh," Laura smiled. "We do admire your loyalty."

"As far as the congregation goes," Grant continued, "I seriously doubt many of them will have a problem with this. They're restless. They want new blood too. I think they want to aim at something a little more realistic and put the old pie-in-the-sky vision behind them."

"Along with anyone who still has that vision?"

"I'm sorry, Josh, but probably."

"Great. Well, I'd rather sink with his ship than jump to another."

"Casualties of war, Josh. Those are the breaks."

+ + + +

We do not live in a patient age. Stockholders press for new leadership when a business sees several quarters go by without an upturn in revenue. Sports fans storm the airwaves with complaints when the coach of their favorite team hasn't put together a winning season in several years. And, in some cases, it takes more than winning seasons to impress them. It takes *impressive* winning seasons—and championships. We want success, and if the people at the helm aren't making it happen, there are plenty of others competing for the chance to try.

Moses knew what it was like to coach a team starved for championships, and he also knew there were plenty of people out there who thought they could do a better job of leading the nation than he was doing. He hadn't even applied for the job; he was chosen by a persuasive search committee consisting of a mysterious voice and a burning bush. But the owner of that voice had shown up in power again and again, and through him, Moses secured the release of a whole race of slaves. A cloud led, a sea parted, an army was drowned, and a wilderness lay ahead. On the other side of that was a promise—a land flowing with milk and honey. The problem was that the milk and honey weren't immediately available. The people of God had to go through some transition years first.

*Transition years never bode well for a leader.*

Transition years never bode well for a leader. That's practically a no-win situation, unless the transition happens to be fast and the success comes quickly. But when you're dealing with a God who's zealous about being thorough, transitions don't go quickly and success has a whole different definition. For a restless, uncooperative crowd, that's a problem.

That's why the Israelites began complaining even before they left Egypt and continued their grumbling almost all the way to the Promised Land. In the interim, God weeded out a generation that refused to believe even after all they had seen. But if God had not stepped in to prove Moses' authority on several occasions, there would have been a full-scale rebellion against him.

Think about that. Here was a leader who had demonstrated in unprecedented ways that God was with him; was known for his remarkable humility; had been on a mountaintop and seen God to the point that his face shone; had emancipated well over a million slaves from the most powerful kingdom in the region; and had selflessly pleaded before God for people who had petty, faithless complaints and who wanted the end result without the trip to get there. And still they weren't satisfied with the leadership they had been given. So they attempted an overthrow.[1]

Israel's complainers would have fit right in with those of us in business, sports, or ministry who think five years is plenty long enough to demonstrate fruitfulness. God's plans rarely mature quickly, but the wait is always worth it. And it takes a patient leader to steward the maturation process. In the Kingdom of God, we call that "wise." In the kingdoms of this world, we call it "incompetent." And more often than not, I think, the church today has the patience one would expect from the kingdoms of this world. If God hasn't provided growth in a ministry, church, marriage, or anything else in three or four years, the wrong people must be involved. They need to be replaced— just like a coach on a sideline who can't put together a winning season.

*God's plans rarely mature quickly, but the wait is always worth it.*

What God defines as patient endurance and laying the right groundwork, the world (and much of the church) defines as a serious lack of leadership. That's tragic because a lot of God-ordained leaders like Moses, who, in his meekness, probably wasn't particularly flashy or commanding as a headman, get pushed out of the way for not being "the pastorly type" or "the kind of leader we need right now" or something along those lines. In other words, we normally wouldn't have agreed with the burning bush. It must have picked the wrong passerby.

We know now, obviously, what God thought of those who challenged

*Destructive criticism targeted at someone whom God has placed in authority is essentially criticism of God.*

Moses' leadership. He was rather demonstrative in his response, opening the ground at one point for the chief complainers to fall into. When God has placed someone in a position of authority, destructive criticism targeted at that person is essentially criticism of God. If we're absolutely convinced that a leader is outside the will of God, then maybe that person is fair game for the normal processes of complaint and possible removal. And accountability and constructive advice are always necessary components of any God-led venture. But it's a serious thing to undermine God's anointed without clear, divine guidance to do so.

We see that truth in Scripture often. God's covenant with his chosen people included a provision to "bless those who bless you" and cursed those who cursed them.[2] Even David, with a clear calling from God to be king and a wicked king standing in his way, refused to raise a hand against God's anointed. It's entirely up to God to put his people in their proper roles and to remove them when necessary. And when that happens to involve a prayerful process initiated by the community of believers, it needs to be carried out without slanderous judgments and harsh criticism. The calling of God is sacred; we challenge it at our own risk.

The reason God is so opposed to those who contend against his chosen leaders should be obvious. In Moses' case, for example, God was working on multiple fronts: weeding out a faithless generation so the Promised Land would be filled with people with faithful hearts;[3] allowing the Canaanites to carry out their depravity until it had run its course and spent God's patience;[4] cultivating Joshua as an effective, godly general; and so on. What statement did the Israelites make when they complained and tried to depose their deliverer? "We don't believe God's promise is going to work out or that he even knows how to follow through on it." Those are slanderous words against the Most High God. On the surface they were directed at Moses, but they hit at the heart of God's plan.

We need to remember that God's plans are being accomplished at multiple levels even when we can't see how. Assuming that a lack of visible progress translates as "somebody's doing something wrong" is spiritually shallow and shortsighted. The truth is that Israel was on the way to the Promised Land even when they were wandering in the opposite direction, because "on the way" in God's eyes involves things like developing character and establishing firm foundations in addition to visible movement. That's just as true in many of our churches and ministries today—and in businesses and families too, for that matter. God doesn't have a "win or else" approach to his people. He doesn't put spiritual coaches and CEOs in place for a few years and then decide they're just not working out when the numbers fall flat. God is more results oriented about things like integrity and faith than he is in strategic initiatives and balance sheets. He'll remove a leader much more quickly for spiritual rebellion than he will for lack of tangible progress.

*The calling of God is sacred; we challenge it at our own risk.*

Sadly, the church has applied many of the dynamics of performance-based, results-oriented assessment to spiritual leadership. The things that matter most to God, scripturally speaking, are qualitative: whether a leader is developing godly character, hearing his voice, following where he leads, and zealously pursuing his Father's heart. But the things that seem to matter most to evangelical institutions and families are quantitative: whether a leader is making visible progress toward stated goals, seeing numbers increase, and in many cases, padding the endowment. That's unfortunate.

Now does that mean that we shouldn't expect our leaders to be good stewards and manage resources well? Or be accountable for diligence and fruitfulness? Obviously not. These are important concerns for spiritual authority figures. Outcomes should be considered as evidence of a leader's effectiveness. But not as a priority, and certainly not at the expense of deeper issues. We have to give God the latitude to prune his people or work out his timing according to his schedule without listening to our protests and accusations. Some plants bloom every year, and some only once at the twilight of their life span. God's people follow the same variety of schedules. Often when we push his processes according to our criteria for growth and progress, we abort or undermine those processes. We demand to pick fruit before it's ripe and then curse the tree for its inefficiency. That grieves God.

The culture of the Christian church cannot be tainted with the flavor of a radio talk show that invites malcontents to call in and complain about their political leaders. We are not sports fans whose ticket purchases grant us the right to boo the team. We are children of a King who says he's in charge even when it looks like he isn't. A culture of complaint looks much too similar to that of the wilderness wanderers. God's children aren't designed to die in the desert.

When you're dissatisfied with your leaders, ask yourself a few questions. Is your dissatisfaction due to your impatience or to their true mismanagement? Does it come from a results-based expectation or a character-based disappointment? Does it really take into consideration the deep spiritual transactions between the leader and his or her God? Or are you making an outside observation without having all the inside details?

These are more than simply questions of efficiency and stewardship. They are matters of God's anointing on specific people for specific tasks. The only thing that matters is whether someone is still sovereignly ordained for the task at hand. If not, words of correction may be necessary. If so, such words may oppose the purposes of God.

### FORGOTTEN MESSAGES FROM MOSES:

+ God loathes complaining—*especially* complaining against his anointed leaders and often "slow-moving" plans.
+ Spiritual leadership is an entirely different affair than other kinds of leadership. It calls for higher accountability, but also more respect and more patience.
+ God defines efficiency much differently than we do. His is an efficiency of inner character, not of outward agendas.

# CHAPTER 14

# INFERIOR MOTIVES

"Just so we don't run out of time this week, shall we get right to it and pick up where we left off last time?"

"Yeah, that's fine. And where was that, exactly?"

"Well, we were talking about how frustrating it is whenever one of your friends announces that she's going to have a baby—and how easily she seemed to get pregnant. How are things this week?"

"Nothing's really changed. I'm still as discouraged as ever."

"Have you been taking the antidepressant your doctor gave you?"

"Yes."

"Good. And have you been practicing what I suggested for you to work on?"

"What, congratulating my baby-factory friends and praying for them?"

"Yes, that. If you can just get to the point of feeling good for others and expressing that to them, you'll be amazed at how you'll be changed on the inside."

"Well, I can't. I just can't bring myself to say things like that. It's too . . . painful."

"I know it's hard, but I think you should at least give it a try. Instead of focusing on what you're missing, focus on how God has blessed them—and on how he's blessed you. After all, you have a great husband who loves you, all your needs are taken care of, and of course God loves you like a precious daughter. You don't really need a child to feel good about your life."

"You don't understand, do you? This is the deepest desire I've ever had. I'll just die if I can't have a baby. Or wish that I *could* die. This isn't just a want, it's a need."

"I know you feel that way. But I think that's part of the problem.

You've staked your entire identity on being a mother. Did you hear yourself just then? You'd rather die than simply be a daughter of God, a wife for your husband, and all the other things God created you for. That's a sure sign that you're wrapped up in a false identity. I've seen it a thousand times; if you'll find your complete satisfaction in God, then maybe one day, when his timing's right, he'll fulfill that desire. But even if he doesn't, it won't be the most tragic thing in the world because you'll be content in him. You have to find your life in him, not in motherhood."

"I don't know how to do that."

"Well, for starters, you'll need to deal with that sense of envy. I've never known God to answer a prayer rooted in jealousy. That's a poor motivation for having a child."

"That's not my only reason for wanting a baby. I've always wanted to be a mother—ever since I was little."

"I know, and that has shaped who you are. But the Bible doesn't define us by our role in life or by our relationships. It defines us by what Jesus has done for us."

"But don't the desires we have come from God in the first place? Doesn't he give them to us?"

"Oooh, be careful there. He *can* do that, of course, but I think it's best to be suspicious of our desires. I have lots of desires that haven't come from God and will never be fulfilled because I, like all of us, have sin and selfishness in me. And even the ones that do come from him have to be submitted to him. When they aren't, they become larger than God to us, and God won't deal with us on those terms. He won't answer our prayers for something we'll love more than him."

"I'm not going to love my baby more than him. But he did promise to answer my prayers and to give me the desires of my heart."

"True, but there are conditions. You can't just throw whatever's on your heart in front of God and insist that he fulfill it. That sets you up for disappointment when he doesn't buy into your agenda. We're supposed to buy into *his* agenda. *Then* we meet some of the conditions for those promises to be fulfilled."

"Actually, I *have* submitted this desire to him, and I've asked him to use it for his glory."

"Well, that's good, but that doesn't guarantee anything. This is a very common problem, by the way. You see, here's what happens: When we have certain expectations that God doesn't fulfill, we grieve and grow depressed. Then we grow bitter and resentful, which leads to more depression, which leads to more bitterness, and so on. And right now, that's the path you're on. We need to work together to get you out of that cycle so you can be happy with wherever God has you right now rather than waiting for the big miracle that will change everything. That's very unrealistic."

"So you don't think he'll answer me if I've dedicated the answer to his glory?"

"What do you mean by that? How do you expect to dedicate your child to his glory?"

"I'm going to offer my baby up to God for his service. As long as I can take care of my baby when he or she is little, then God can have him or her for life."

"Oh, dear . . . I see so many things in there that aren't healthy for you. One, that tells me that maybe your desire isn't so much to raise a child as it is to be labeled a mother. That's a status or role issue that's very deeply rooted in some of your insecurities. And we've talked about that before, remember? When you first started coming to me. Somehow you got the message, maybe from your mother, that womanhood is all about having children, and that you really aren't a complete 'woman' until you've given birth. And that's just not true at all. That's a false picture of what it means to be a woman."

"I know, I know. We've talked about that a lot. I don't know if that's the message my mother gave me, but I guess that idea is in me somewhere."

"In the second place, that kind of vow doesn't really take into account the gifts and calling and interests of your child. Don't you think he or she would want some say in what it means to follow God? What if your child wants to be an architect or a writer or something? Maybe that will be his or her calling, which really isn't any different from the way a lot of people serve God. I don't think God wants you to determine the course of your child's life based on your desperation to be a mother."

"Well, I don't mean that he, or maybe she, would have to be a career minister. I just mean that he'll be totally sold out to God in whatever he does."

"Okay, I can see that. But my concern here is that you seem to be making a deal with God in order to get your way—bargaining with him like maybe you can twist his arm. Does that sound biblical to you? Or very spiritually mature?"

"I guess not."

"Right. That's a very human tendency—a temptation for all of us. I don't think you're intentionally trying to manipulate God, of course. But that's basically what this is. You're trying to create some leverage to use with him."

"I didn't think of it that way."

"Don't worry, there's no shame in that. We all have to learn what spiritually mature praying is like. I think biblical prayer is asking God according to his will and then accepting his answer, whatever it happens to be. And then being able to trust him to do what's best for you."

"I guess I know that. I'm just so . . . frustrated. I'm desperate, you know?"

"Yes, I know. It's hard when we don't have all the answers. But I can promise you that God knows what he's doing, and he loves you very much. Now, do you want to meet at the same time again next week?"

"Okay."

"Next time I'd like to focus more on handling the depression side of this issue rather than talking about the issue itself, okay? And don't stop taking the medication the doctor prescribed; it takes a while before anything starts to change. Just keep at it."

+ + + +

Hannah's story isn't idealized in Scripture. She was one of two wives of Elkanah—the wife he loved more, in fact. But in spite of his tremendous affection for her, she felt slighted. God had not given her any children, while her rival had borne many. In a culture in which God had emphasized inheritance—a Promised Land passed down from generation to generation along paternal lines—children were more than just bundles of joy. They were a sacred legacy.

The fact that Elkanah's other wife had children stirred up intense jealousy in Hannah. She cried often. She had no appetite. Her rival made snide remarks just to irritate her, and it worked. In a moment of prayer,

Hannah poured out her heart to God so passionately that she appeared drunk and unstable. Tears covered her face and she seemed to be mouthing nonsense. She was in great "bitterness of soul" (1 Samuel 1:10). So she made a radical vow—a deal with God—to offer up her child to his service if he ever gave her a child to offer.

The scenario above describes how a counselor might respond to someone like Hannah, but the conversation really doesn't need to take place in a clinical setting. It could happen between any two friends. Imagine someone you know being so envious of pregnant women that she promises to give up her child for adoption if God will just give her one to raise for about three years. Does that sound healthy and balanced to you? I didn't think so.

No, Hannah may have had some pure motives for wanting a baby, but those motives were mixed with envy and a strong sense of competition. She didn't consider herself blessed by God unless she could bear children. Her husband's deep love for her wasn't enough. Neither was her relationship with God. She wanted a baby at all costs.

That's enough to keep a counselor busy for years. I've known several women who were desperate to have children, and their desperation, while very understandable, has always been viewed as an emotional symptom to be treated, not a spiritual asset to be cultivated. That's because we—society in general and evangelicals in particular—believe that severe emotional distress is a sign of immaturity and dysfunction. We rarely, if ever, see it as God's means to accomplish his will.

Not only would we frown on Hannah's envy and competitiveness, we'd tell her how inappropriate it is to try to bargain with God. It isn't our place to twist his arm—that's childish and unspiritual. It's an attempt to manipulate God to fit our own agenda rather than submitting our will to his. We've even gone so far as telling people that God won't answer prayers that come from impure motives or that attempt to buy his favor with unrealistic promises. Sometimes we've called such attempts "paganism" or "idolatry of self" or even "witchcraft." That kind of prayer seems so . . . unholy.

It's true that wrong motives can hinder our prayers[1] and that God's favor can't be bought,[2] but in his mercy, he often answers petitions based on mixed motives and offered vows. It's clear, for example, that many desperate prayers in the Psalms were not purely for the glory of the Lord; at times, the people praying simply wanted to win a battle or save their own skin. It isn't that they weren't concerned for God's glory, but the driving force behind their prayers wasn't always completely selfless. So why did God answer? Because he interacts with us at our points of need—mercifully, graciously, lovingly. Selfish prayers may not be answered very often, but prayers born from self-interest often are.

> *In his mercy, God often answers petitions based on mixed motives and offered vows.*

God answered Hannah's prayer, of course. It's recorded in 1 Samuel 1–2, and the song of gratitude she sings in chapter 2 is one of the most beautiful praises in Scripture, comparable to Mary's Magnificat in Luke 1:46-55. Isn't that amazing? Apparently, God wasn't aware at that time that envious prayers and desperate vows were spiritually immature and didn't deserve a response. For some reason, he responded anyway.

You won't find Hannah's prayer of desperation in any of our "how to pray" books—though you are likely to find certain *parts* of her prayer of thanksgiving when she brought Samuel to the Tabernacle: how God had planted a need in her heart through which he'd bring forth a godly priest; how God is attentive to our desperate pleas; and how she sought God's glory above all and sacrificed her son to his service. But the first prayer that exposed her envy, her provocation, her unbalanced emotions, and her bargaining—that's just not exemplary enough. God won't answer prayers that have so much baggage behind them. Except he did.

Our typical assessment of Hannah's prayer is a prime example of how we sterilize the experiences of biblical heroes. Their motives and behaviors are a mixed bag of godliness and self, so we purify them. We have to; we don't know how to explain a holy God who seems to tacitly endorse less-than-holy approaches to him. Those approaches *must* have been pure. So we clean them up to fit our theology.

Why are we so intent on idealizing biblical characters? Because the discrepancy between their experience with God and ours has to be explained somehow. Our religious instincts tell us that God blesses those who measure up, and that those who *really* measure up are blessed even more extravagantly. If people like Hannah received amazing miracles from God, then people like Hannah must be supersaints. And if we can be supersaints too, then we can experience the same kinds of miracles they did. Our interpretation of them fits our expectations, not their reality.

The startling fact is that in the Bible, God more often does miracles for weak, humble, and unassuming people who cry out and admit their brokenness to him than he does for those normally considered holy and righteous and theologically mature. He's much more responsive to honest dysfunction than to beautiful but dishonest masks. We forget that, so we put beautiful masks on flawed characters in Scripture. We forget the flaws of these biblical heroes because we can't

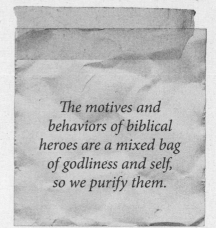

*The motives and behaviors of biblical heroes are a mixed bag of godliness and self, so we purify them.*

come to grips with the fact that the only prerequisite to a miracle is radical faith in God. It just doesn't seem appropriate for spiritually incompetent people to get God's blessings. And even if we did understand that dynamic intellectually, we'd have a hard time wholeheartedly striving to get low enough for his blessing.

Try to imagine how the Hannah dynamic would play out today in the following situations. How would you react to

+ A CEO who pleads with God to gain a greater share of the market than a rival company—and he'll give half of his personal profits to missions.
+ A man who promises that if God lets him marry the woman he desperately loves, he'll go to seminary and learn how to begin a ministry for married couples.
+ A student who vows that if God happens to bless her with an A in her hardest course, she'll commit to tutor kids in the projects for an hour each week—at least until next semester.

These cases generally prompt a negative reaction in us. Why? Because they seem somewhat self-centered, maybe even mercenary. Where was the commitment to God's glory before the need arose? Why wasn't the CEO already giving to missions out of his huge profits? If the desperate romantic feels called to start a ministry for couples, why doesn't he just be obedient and do it? If the student really has a heart for kids in the projects, why hasn't she been tutoring them? And if she hasn't been working with them, why does she think God would give her an A and put her there? Generosity toward God and a desire to earn achievements rather than plead for gifts should be part and parcel of the Christian life. These prayers don't seem to come from spiritually mature people.

But these are exactly the kind of prayers God has answered in the past—and that he answered for Hannah. If we try to hyperspiritualize our prayer life, we'll miss the generosity of God because we'll always think he answered because we measured up. But God doesn't pour out his grace solely on people who measure up. That's why it's called "grace"—unmerited favor. Our religious instincts care a lot more about being spiritual than about being real. And God is always looking for real.

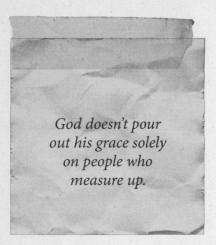

*God doesn't pour out his grace solely on people who measure up.*

That doesn't mean, of course, that he answers every real prayer the way we expect him to. It does, however, mean that he prefers to communicate with us in very honest terms, and that he doesn't disqualify us from answers simply because our prayers aren't "spiritual" enough. But he loves authenticity in our prayers, even when authenticity reveals mixed motives.

That's the reason he answered Hannah's prayer, in my opinion. She was real with her need and never attempted to base her appeal on her innocence or worthiness to get her desire met. In fact, God often seems to use our desperation to set up his plans. When he's planning to show his people his power to save, he lets them suffer a need to be saved. When he wants to demonstrate his willingness to hear our cries, he allows us to cry. Through our intense longings and desires, he paves the way for his provision. That's what he did with an envious, desperate housewife in the Promised Land long ago. She cried out for something personal, and he delivered it for a larger purpose. And a nation's history was changed.

## FORGOTTEN MESSAGES FROM HANNAH:

+ Severe emotional distress could be a symptom of a problem, but it could also be the means God has chosen to bring us to our knees to accomplish his purposes.
+ Some of our intense desires were put into our hearts by God himself.
+ God often answers our prayers even when our motives aren't pure—which, considering how often complete purity eludes us, is welcome news.

# THAT LOOKS WEIRD

I'M SURROUNDED BY FOOLS, and for that I'm thankful. That's because fools qualify for a distinct honor: they can demonstrate the foolishness of God and shame the wisdom of this world.[1] And not only are fools perfectly fit for the Kingdom of God, so are weaklings. Anyone lacking in strength is a prime candidate for displaying God's power.[2] It seems that God doesn't always honor our sense of dignity or our rigorous education. He doesn't mind those attributes in someone with enough maturity to realize how much he or she doesn't need them, but Scripture makes it clear that God often uses ridiculous means to reveal himself.

Just ask Balaam's donkey, or the one that carried Jesus into Jerusalem. They might have embarrassed the world's greatest kings, but they greatly honored the ultimate King. God gets glory even—or especially—from odd-looking beasts.

That's the way of the Lord. If a message comes in sophisticated and dignified clothing, it probably isn't from him. But if the message looks weird, defies social standards, and stretches our comfort zone—if it leaves us scratching our heads and wondering how something so seemingly fruitful but strangely packaged could possibly be from God—it just might be. "Weird" is not a valid test of whether something is godly or not. In fact, it's often God's preferred mode of communication.

✦ ✦ ✦ ✦

# CHAPTER 15

# DELUSIONAL FAITH

"What do you think of them?" Bruce asked, turning the conversation to a more serious subject. He set his coffee down and leaned back.

"Who, the old couple who've been coming?"

"Yeah, the old couple."

"Very strange," said Gary.

"Yeah, thanks. Everybody knows that. Give me more. You know how I trust your judgment."

"Well, I appreciate that. But I'm at a loss on this one. Don't they teach you about this kind of thing in seminary?"

"Um, no. Not really. Or maybe I just missed that day."

Gary smiled. "Can't you, as their pastor, refer them to a psychiatrist or a state agency or something?"

"You mean give them a phone number and tell them to call for help? Somehow I think they wouldn't go for that. In fact, they'd be pretty offended."

"Maybe that's not such a bad thing."

"C'mon, Gary. Be serious."

"I *am* serious. They'd just go find another church, and then you and the rest of us wouldn't have to deal with them."

"Please. I didn't miss *that* day at seminary. We're in the business of helping people, not pawning them off on other churches."

"I know your heart, Bruce, and I admire you for it. But seriously, do you really think you can help them? Isn't that just a tad unrealistic? I don't think they're open to it, or even that they think they need help. They're too far gone."

"I think at some level they know they're not normal, don't you?"

"Probably. But to them there's nothing wrong with 'not normal,' you know? It's almost like a badge of honor. Makes them feel special, I guess."

"Okay, let me ask you this, then. Let's say we just let them go on with their delusion. They can go on telling everyone God's going to give them a child, everyone can keep pretending to smile, and life will go on."

"Bruce, they're old. I mean *really* old. Like ludicrously old."

"Right. Obviously I'm not saying it's true. I'm just saying what's wrong with letting them believe that?"

"Because when they finally realize it isn't going to happen, they'll have a major crisis of faith on their hands—and on your hands, too, once they come to their pastor and ask you to help them explain it. Decades of delusion can't be cleaned up with a few hours of counseling. Then you'll *have* to refer them to someone else. Besides, it just isn't healthy."

"What do you mean, 'when they realize it won't happen'? They've hung on to it this long. I'm pretty sure it isn't going to suddenly hit them that it's a ridiculous thought. People don't grow more sane as they get older, you know? And honestly that's a blessing, especially in their case. I think the day they realize it isn't going to happen is the day they wake up in heaven and see things as they really are. And as weird as I think they are, I do think they're going to heaven. They'll be with Jesus, and those unfulfilled dreams won't even cross their mind. And in the meantime, they're not really hurting anyone."

"Well, maybe . . . unless you count the visitors who didn't come back because they talked to 'the crazy old couple.' I don't think our people are going to humor them much longer."

Both men sipped on their coffee for a minute before Gary broke the silence. "What do you think happened? How do people get like that?"

"I don't know. They must have been so desperate to have a child that they convinced themselves God was going to give them one. And then when they got past the age for that, they just didn't give up their faith. Probably told themselves things like, 'Faith sees beyond circumstances,' and 'All things are possible with God.' You know, the stuff I preach all the time to people who know I'm not giving them permission to believe absurd and bizarre things like this. Makes me wonder . . . do I have to offer a disclaimer with every sermon?"

"It seems like at some point in time, someone would have pulled them aside and said, 'You know, folks, there comes a point when it's time to let go of a dream. For whatever reason, God didn't allow you to have kids. That doesn't make you less of a couple. He obviously has other plans for you. Whatever regrets you've had in your past, you need to put them behind you and move on.'"

"I'm sure someone did. Probably lots of people. But for whatever reason, they just couldn't accept it."

"Can you imagine, though? Even if they did have a child, how in the world do they think they could take care of one? How old are they?"

"I don't know exactly. I don't think anyone's ever asked them. At least in their eighties, I'd guess."

"See, this isn't just a simple deception in one area. It's more than the fact that it would take a miracle to get pregnant. They couldn't handle it—physically, mentally, emotionally, whatever. It would kill them. Not that they aren't going to die in a few years anyway. And then where would the child go?"

Another pause, another sip. Bruce sighed. "You know what really bothers me, Gary?"

"Hmm?"

"They're practicing what most preachers preach. Like I said, this is what we encourage people to believe."

"No way. Don't be ridiculous. I've never heard you encourage this."

"No, I don't mean to this extreme. But isn't it really the logical conclusion of what we teach about faith? I mean, where do you draw the line and say, 'Oh, no, that's not what I meant. Most of what you believe isn't too impossible for God, but this is'?"

"That's not the point. It isn't that this is impossible for God. Nothing's impossible for him. That's not what we're talking about. We're talking about stuff that obviously isn't his will. I'm pretty sure he doesn't want an eighty-something couple to have a kid. And he certainly doesn't want us to live in a fantasy world."

"True, Gary. That's very true. But he also wants us to have faith that he can do the unexpected."

"Okay, look at it this way. What are their motives? Clearly they have some incredibly inflated need to find their identity in a child. Kind of like they can't be real people unless they're parents. It's sad and it's sick. I've heard you preach about our true identity plenty of times, and you've been clear that people don't need a spouse, child, career, or whatever else to be fulfilled. They need God, right? And then I've also heard you preach about contentment more times than I can count. Obviously, they aren't content. So, yeah, technically their faith is reaching out for the impossible. But you have to balance that with being content with what you have."

"Yeah, I know. But that can be a really hard balance to find."

"Maybe so, but they aren't even close. They crossed that line a long time ago, long before they ever got to us. I may not know exactly how to balance those things, but I know enough to know that these folks are way out of balance."

"Obviously. And I don't mean to play the devil's advocate—I know they're mentally off as well as you do. But I do have a hard time putting my finger on exactly what's wrong with what they're hoping for. I mean, I'm sure it's not God's will for them. But exactly how to prove that from Scripture . . . I'm not sure."

"Well, I don't think you have to prove something like that from Scripture. God gave us brains so we could use them. There's nothing in the Bible about ignoring good old common sense. But I understand what you're saying. You feel sorry for them. You've got a pastor's heart. That's a good thing, remember? It's okay, I feel sorry for them too." Gary winked. "I just think they're wacko."

+ + + +

When I was young, I didn't hear many people say, "The Lord told me . . ." and then fill in the blank with an instruction or a promise. That wasn't very common in the church I grew up in. But whenever people did say God had told them something, it sounded impressive and somewhat mysterious. I thought that was pretty cool.

Fascination turned to skepticism in my teens. Many claims of hearing God's instructions or promises in a specific situation seemed a little eccentric or unGod-like. I thought some of them even crossed the line into delusion and selfishness. And since my church discouraged that sort of thing, I came to believe that the more specific a claim was, the less likely it was to be from God. And the more extravagant and unrealistic the claim seemed to be, the greater the delusion involved.

I held that perspective for many years, and it's still part of me. I think a fair dose of skepticism can be healthy—to a point. Discernment is a good thing. But the danger in that attitude is that it can easily turn a deaf ear to the voice of God. We settle into an expectation that if God is going to move among us, his voice will sound reasonable and the wind of his Spirit will blow in conventional directions. And that is a decidedly unbiblical assumption.

There are plenty of examples of God working through eccentric people and, in fact, initiating the very eccentricities we remember them for. Abraham and Sarah are one of the most interesting among those examples. God told Abraham that he would be blessed with many descendants, but his wife was barren. As it turns out, she would continue to be barren for at least the next couple of decades. In the painful interim between promise and fulfillment, the couple used Sarah's maid as a surrogate mother. After all, if God had spoken this promise, he'd certainly need a plausible means of giving Abraham children, right? Obviously not, as the results of the well-known story make clear. God would bless the maid's son, Ishmael, as a child of Abraham, but that wasn't the son that was promised. That son, Isaac, would come at a time so ludicrously "late" that Sarah laughed at the divine visitor who promised her motherhood within a year. A child in their old age? Ridiculous. It was too late. She was years, even decades, past childbearing age. She would have looked foolish hanging on to such an absurd hope.

> *We expect that if God is going to move among us, his voice will sound reasonable and the wind of his Spirit will blow in conventional directions. That is a decidedly unbiblical assumption.*

But the Bible is full of absurd hopes and predictions. Building an ark on dry land because God said it would rain a lot one day? Raising a staff over an enormous body of water to make an escape route through it? Marching around a city so its walls would fall down? The list could go on and on and on, and every item on that list would look ridiculous if we encountered them in our own experience. If a man told us he had divine instructions to build a massive, seaworthy ship in the middle of Nebraska because of a coming global flood, he'd be the butt of jokes at the office. If we found ourselves at the edge of Lake Michigan with a horde of angry, well-armed barbarians breathing down our necks, we'd complain about the impossibility of crossing the water on a path of dry land just as vehemently as the Israelites did at the Red Sea. If our president held a press conference informing us that our new military strategy when taking a city would be to march thousands of our soldiers around it for seven days, the headlines would be full of calls for impeachment on grounds of mental incompetence. In all of these cases and more, we'd oppose the work of God. Like Sarah, we'd laugh.

Faith looks heroic in hindsight, once all the results are in. In the present, it often looks utterly foolish. From God's perspective, the more absurd his voice sounds, the greater faith we'll need to believe it. He is honored more by great faith than by reasonable faith, so his absurdities are a wonderful opportunity for his people. But from the ground level where we see everything, a claim to have heard ridiculous instructions and promises is a sign of senility, not sainthood. In our minds, there's nothing heroic about the couple in the conversation above.

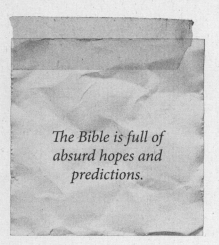

*The Bible is full of absurd hopes and predictions.*

How is this relevant to us today? Well, when God wants to do a miracle— heal a disease, repair a broken family, save a loved one, fulfill an impossible desire—he often cultivates our faith by promising it to us ahead of time and causing us to wait for it. During the wait, our faith gets thrown into a crucible along with our rational processes, our own sense of dignity, our doctrinal assumptions, the opinions of others, our history of disappointment or unbelief, our distractions, and our unwillingness to endure long trials. If, after intense flames under that crucible, the last element remaining is our faith, then we've matured spiritually by leaps and bounds; and God is honored. He comes out ahead in that competitive stew, and our hearts have become pure. And that, more often than not, is when miracles come.

Most Christians, however, let our faith lose. God's promises don't survive the buildup of mistrust, dignified religion, rationalism, doctrines, past disappointments, and fickleness of our hearts. His promises always win when we let them, but we've been trained in the art of suspicion for too many years. So we believe the heroic faith of people in the Bible—that's easy, because we see how God came through in their lives—but we don't believe the absurd faith of the quirky people around us. In matters of faith, there's a fine line between admirable and asinine, and we can't see that line until after the story resolves. So even when the verdict is still out on a claim of "God told me . . . ," we go ahead and make our judgment on it.

> *Faith looks heroic in hindsight, once all the results are in. In the present, it often looks utterly foolish.*

I'm certainly not advocating a blind acceptance of all the claims we hear. There really are deluded or self-centered people out there who just want to be able to say God told them something, even when he didn't. But assuming that a person is off his or her rocker right away is unnecessary. We can ask God if he's behind what they're claiming. We can respond to a bizarre belief with noncommittal interest: "Oh really? I'll be interested to see how God works through that situation." And then wait and see.

If we want to be really biblical, that's exactly the kind of attitude we'll need to have. We can't determine if something is truly God-ordained or not by how absurd or impossible it is. Those are not scriptural criteria for the work of God. When God gives us his instructions or his promises, words like *flaky, bizarre, impossible, weird,* and *offensive* are completely irrelevant. The only criterion we're biblically allowed to use is whether something is consistent with the character and the purposes of God. And even on this point, we need to embrace a certain level of humility and acknowledge how incompletely we see him.

When an Abraham and Sarah make a ridiculous claim to us, they might be divinely appointed for a particular purpose. Or they might be frauds. We don't have to decide which—no one really set us up as judge in that situation. We need to be alert against false doctrine, but we often can't determine whether someone has had a false experience. If we feel compelled to assess someone's claim, however, we need to be open to the possibility that God just might be up to the kinds of things he did in the Bible. Otherwise, we might find ourselves denying a work God himself has begun.

**FORGOTTEN MESSAGES FROM ABRAHAM AND SARAH:**

+ Some people who claim that God told them something are right. Some are wrong. It's dangerous to try to decide which is which when we have no stake in the matter.

+ "Insane," "embarrassing," and "impossible" are not valid criteria for determining the will of God.

+ The Bible never commands us to make a decision about someone else's claims, as long as they are consistent with the clearly revealed aspects of God's character and purposes. It's okay to wait and see or to say, "I don't know."

# CHAPTER 16

# HARD LABOR

*Support group session at the Christian Career Center at Crosspath Community Church:*

**CAREER COUNSELOR:** Welcome back, folks. As you'll recall from last week, we talked about how God calls us and discussed some things to look for to help us discover that call. This week I want us to look at the results of those assessment tools you filled out last week and see what they might reveal about God's will for you. You don't have to share your results with the group if you don't want to, of course, but I thought it might be helpful if we could talk through these things with two or three of you so we can get an idea of how to use these tools. I know you haven't had much time to look them over, but does anyone want to volunteer to start?

**LIZ:** I will.

**COUNSELOR:** Great! What did you discover about yourself?

**LIZ:** This says I'm a detail person who would do well working with statistics or accounts. Except it also says I'm creative and need to express my individuality.

**COUNSELOR:** Did you already know this about yourself?

**LIZ:** Sure, sort of. But I'm not sure how to reconcile those two things.

**COUNSELOR:** Remind me, what kind of work are you doing now?

**LIZ:** I work at Starbucks.

**COUNSELOR:** Oh, yeah, that's right. And you're looking for something to pay the bills while you explore . . . what was it? Acting?

**LIZ:** Yeah.

**COUNSELOR:** Hmmm. Well, there are two ways to go about that. You can fulfill those two sides of yourself in two separate activities—a job in accounting, for example, and creative pursuits on the side—or blending the two in your work, which would be more ideal. Does it list any options for you?

**LIZ:** A few. I'll have to think about them.

**COUNSELOR:** Okay, let's come back to that. Who else?

**JERRY:** My situation is a little different because I already know I'm doing what God has called me to do. But it doesn't fit me very well, and I want to see if there are some ways to make it more satisfying.

**COUNSELOR:** Sure, we can do that. But let's put your current situation mentally on hold for a few minutes. I'm glad you're confident that you're doing what God has called you to do, but it might be helpful to keep an open mind while we talk about it—especially if you think it doesn't fit you very well. What does your assessment say about you?

**JERRY:** Well, I'm not a people person. My personality is suited more toward research and study, something where I can work independently at my own pace and not be in a highly structured environment. I also need to be surrounded by people who can encourage me without micromanaging me.

**COUNSELOR:** Great! And what do you do now?

**JERRY:** I'm a preacher.

**COUNSELOR:** Oh, really? So you're a little out of your comfort zone, perhaps. What kind of church do you pastor?

**JERRY:** Well, I'm not a pastor. And I don't have a church. I just preach wherever I feel led. Sometimes in churches, sometimes just on the street or in the courthouse square.

**COUNSELOR:** Oh . . . right. Were you by any chance on the news a few weeks ago?

**JERRY:** Yeah, that was probably me.

**COUNSELOR:** And you believe this is what God has called you to do?

**JERRY:** I'm positive.

**COUNSELOR:** And how much do you get paid for that?

**JERRY:** I don't.

**COUNSELOR:** So . . . how do you get by?

**JERRY:** My father's a pastor, so he helps me out sometimes. Then when I'm in jail, they feed me, of course.

**COUNSELOR:** Are you seeing any results from your hard work?

**JERRY:** No, and God told me I wouldn't. But this is my mission anyway.

**COUNSELOR:** And you find this satisfying?

**JERRY:** No, not at all. I'm miserable. I wish I could do something else, but God told me to do this. I don't see how I can go on doing it. But at the same time, I don't see how I can not go on doing it.

**COUNSELOR:** Okay, maybe this would be a good time as a group to go over some of those principles we talked about last week. Anyone remember the first one? God's calling is going to be consistent with the way he made us, right? Our gifts, talents, skills, and interests all come into play there. He didn't gift you in one area and then call you to another. Then, even though all jobs have their ups and downs and some seasons when things are not so great, overall the work God designed us for should be satisfying. He didn't create us to be miserable all the time, right? Next—and again, there will be dry seasons, so this is a general statement—over the course of our lives, our work for him will be fruitful. As we partner with him to accomplish his purposes, he lets us see some of the results of what we've done. Finally, God leads us through opportunities. He will open doors for the things he wants us to do. If we keep running into closed doors, it's usually time to reconsider whether we've heard his guidance correctly because he doesn't lead us to live in futility. So as a group, let's apply this to Jerry's situation. Anyone have any suggestions for how he can find God's will for his work?

**JERRY:** But I already know I'm doing what God told me to do. It was very, very clear. And really, his words are so overwhelming in me, I don't think I can do anything else. It's actually painful not to do this.

**COUNSELOR**: But it also seems really painful to continue doing it, and so something must be off in terms of understanding God's will. Or maybe he called you to do this just for a short time and now wants to lead you to something more satisfying.

**JERRY**: No, I'm pretty sure it's for life.

**COUNSELOR**: Let me ask you this: How do the people close to you feel about your calling? You mentioned your dad helping you out with your financial situation. Are your friends and the rest of your family supportive?

**JERRY**: Not really. Some of them hate what I do. A couple of years ago, some people from my hometown plotted to kill me. I think a couple of my brothers were in on it too.

**COUNSELOR**: Are you serious?

**JERRY**: Yeah . . . weird, isn't it?

**COUNSELOR**: Um, that's a little more than weird. Could you prove that if you had to? Was anyone ever arrested for it?

**JERRY**: No, I didn't have time or money to try to prosecute. Or the desire, either. It would have been a distraction.

**COUNSELOR**: Have you thought about how impossible this kind of work will be whenever you decide to get married and have a family?

**JERRY**: Oh, that won't happen. It's forbidden. God says that would be a distraction too. Plus, I think my life is supposed to illustrate judgment and tragedy. I don't think a wife fits in the picture.

**COUNSELOR**: Okay, I'm not sure we need to spend any more time on this as a group, but will you check with me afterward to set up a time to talk about some of these things privately and in more detail?

**JERRY**: Okay, sure.

+ + + +

When I was in college, a street preacher used to come to campus every year for a week. He would stand in the square and shout out his message, which was generally harsh and judgmental. The non-Christians on campus ridiculed this guy relentlessly, and the student newspaper regularly made jokes about his "antics" during the week he was there. Christian students weren't very happy when he came to town either because he gave us a bad name and portrayed a different picture of God than what we tried to represent. We understood that his message was in the mold of Old Testament prophecy, although only partially, as even the harshest of prophets ended with messages of hope and restoration. But we hated the negative attention that this kind of preaching brought on Christianity and knew, despite the many ways we distanced ourselves from his brand of faith, that this was how others perceived us.

In many ways, Jeremiah's ministry evoked these kinds of responses in his listeners. He preached righteousness and impending judgment in the days before Babylon sacked Jerusalem, destroyed the Temple, and carried the chosen people off into captivity. But few people really believed God would allow this—they were unaware of the depths of their sin and insensitive to God's voice—so Jeremiah's opponents ridiculed him and persecuted him with insults, prison, and death threats. Even the godly who remained in Jerusalem weren't very comfortable with his message. It was discouraging and harsh, and there wasn't anything immediately hopeful in it. It gave God's redemptive nature a bad name.

But in spite of the fact that the godly and ungodly alike were resistant to Jeremiah's preaching, God had inspired it. This was Jeremiah's calling. It didn't fit his personality and skills, humanly speaking, and it certainly didn't seem very emotionally or spiritually healthy. He was caught between two dreadful options: preaching and suffering the fire of opposition, or not preaching and suffering the fire in his bones. Either way, his life was miserable. To this day, he's called "the weeping prophet."

That's because God formed this man's life to represent his grief. That was his design, even while Jeremiah was in the womb. His bones would be formed to burn with the pangs of judgment. His calling was to declare the wrath of God on people who would hate him for it. God's people had continued to commit spiritual adultery by worshiping idols and ruling unjustly, even after God had sent prophet upon prophet to warn them to stop. Jeremiah received the divine privilege of being born to declare that it was over. The time for repentance had passed; judgment would come. He would ultimately live to witness the merciless destruction of the holy city at the hands of a vast Babylonian army. Why? So he could stand in the desolate rubble and write heart-wrenching laments to the glory of God.

If that were your calling, how would you feel about God? More than that, how do you think the Christians around you would feel about your calling? Do you think they would be supportive? Or would you be as shunned and ridiculed as the guy who used to come to my campus every year?[1]

Obviously, this kind of calling would not go over well in many Christian circles. Jeremiah would not be welcome in many of our churches, and even those that did welcome him would tire of him quickly. The prophetic ministry, Old Testament style, is not very appealing.

The typical response to that claim is that we aren't in Old Testament times anymore. "That wouldn't happen now because the situation is different," I've heard people say. "We live after the Cross." But that's really not the point, is it? Even after the Cross, God has warned of final judgment, and he never disavowed the possibility of sending some of his servants to warn about it. But even if he had, it's clear that it was in God's heart a long time ago to destine a man for lifelong misery to make a point.[2] And when something comes out of an unchanging heart, that heart is capable of doing the same thing again. We have to wrestle with the fact that the pain of Jeremiah's calling was and is consistent with God's character. It's true that because he poured out his wrath on his innocent Son, who was judged in our place, God doesn't judge his people with ultimate punishment. But he still disciplines his people—the Babylonian captivity was essentially discipline, not divorce—and he still allows many of his godly ones to undergo extreme suffering.[3]

*We have to wrestle with the fact that the pain of Jeremiah's calling was and is consistent with God's character.*

Look at this from God's point of view. If he wanted to send his church a message of repentance, how do you think he would go about it? We know the message wouldn't be comfortable for us because repentance never is. That's especially true when someone else is pointing out our flaws—and God's messages almost always come through a person.[4] When people are preaching negative things, we usually assume that they're operating in the flesh rather than in the Spirit because God wouldn't be so confrontational, would he? So can you conceive of any means God would use to get our attention and turn us around that *wouldn't* get on our nerves? I can't either. I believe any Old Testament prophet in any modern church would be about as popular as Martin Luther at the Vatican.

But with nearly three millennia separating us from Jeremiah and his colleagues, we revere their prophetic writings and conduct Bible studies on them. (Although the studies on Jeremiah still aren't flying off the bookshelves as quickly as the studies on other books.) It's the same old phenomenon of embracing correction when it's far enough removed from our lives and bristling at it when it gets too close.

Words aside, though, the person of Jeremiah wouldn't be considered very godly today. Consider these unappealing facts:

+ He was visibly depressed most of the time. We'd call him a tormented soul.
+ His writings and ministry were fragmented to the point that scholars still can't determine their exact chronology. He jumped from present to past to future and back again without much warning—a reflection of scattered thoughts and fractured emotions.
+ He seemed morbidly introspective.
+ He was generally timid and hated conflict.
+ His belief that God had designated him for a special task that no one else would accept is evidence (to us) of narcissism and a perverse desire for negative attention.
+ He was somewhat reclusive and had few friends, if any, other than his scribe, Baruch.[5]
+ He wouldn't listen to the advice of others because he was convinced that he was right about God's voice and everyone else was wrong. That, of course, violated a clear scriptural principle that there's wisdom in the counsel of many.[6]
+ Even though he was convinced God had spoken, he accused God of deceiving him[7] and the people of Judah.[8] If someone today accused God of being deceitful, the outcry would be deafening.

+ He appeared to be obsessed with God's wrath and judgment.
+ His ministry was almost completely fruitless. There's little evidence of anyone responding positively to his message and repenting.
+ He had several issues career counselors would have jumped on, including a serious lack of boundaries between ministry and personal life; an inability to accept the idea that God would want him in more effective and rewarding work; and a perception that God might not want him to be happy in any area of life.
+ He died in misery, possibly at the hands of the people he aimed to serve.

I think we would have a lot of counsel for Jeremiah. We would tell him that God's ultimate purpose for him is joy[9] and that God has ordained satisfaction in his work.[10] We'd suggest that his long-term fruitlessness is a clear indication that he's not in the right field of work. We'd tell him he's on dangerous ground when he doesn't pay attention to the advice of counselors who point out that God isn't nearly as judgmental and unloving as Jeremiah seems to think he is. We'd argue that his bitter accusations of God deceiving him are a sure sign of having misunderstood God's voice. Because of his personality and anger issues, we might tell him he should consider writing novels or joining a Christian punk rock band instead of struggling with a preaching ministry.

I can recall actual advice I've been given or have given to others that, when applied to Jeremiah, would have opposed God's will. "God never intended for you to be miserable all the time; when a timid person seeks this much negative attention, it's usually a sign of some deep wounds, perhaps an overcompensation for a painfully introverted personality; if you're in God's will, you will eventually bear fruit"; and so on and so on. But in all our blabbering about what God would and wouldn't do and what God wants and doesn't want, we'd be off base with Jeremiah and anyone else in our lives as enigmatic as he was.

Whether we can explain it or not—and we really shouldn't feel like we have to—the God who promises to fulfill the desires of those who love him and who says he'll withhold no good thing from those who walk uprightly is the same God who ordained a life of torment for one of his most faithful servants. Like a good shepherd, he makes his sheep lie down in green pastures; but Jeremiah was thrown into a cistern, endured vicious public ridicule, and barely survived conspiracies to kill him.

So what does Jeremiah's life show us about living a godly life? For one thing, depression isn't necessarily a sign of being out of step with God's Spirit. There are a lot of reasons for depression, and one of them certainly is an ungodly approach to life that seeks to fill our hearts in ways God never intended. Sin has wreaked havoc on the human psyche, and some degree of depression or delusion is almost always the result. But sometimes godly people weep over the brokenness of creation and humanity because life in a fallen world can be sad and even devastating. Anyone filled with God's Spirit instinctively knows something's wrong in much of what we see around us. When God has made someone acutely sensitive to that brokenness, it can be very discouraging. And when God warns of coming disaster,[11] whoever hears the warning becomes either insensitive and detached or deeply grieved.

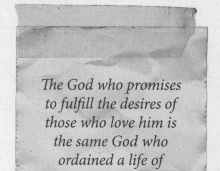

*The God who promises to fulfill the desires of those who love him is the same God who ordained a life of torment for one of his most faithful servants.*

Second, God's calling doesn't always lead us to effective, satisfying, and enjoyable work. I believe it usually does—this is a case where a principle can be a helpful generalization to guide us without being uniformly true—but there are times when God allows his people to carry heavy burdens for the sake of his purposes in this world. This would be true of martyrs, those who live and minister in refugee camps and war zones, and anyone serving where winters seem to last for most of the year. (A few evangelicals might consider the last example an overstatement, though it is widely accepted across denominations.) In general, work is designed for our satisfaction:

> Here is what I have seen to be good and fitting: to eat, to drink
> and enjoy oneself in all one's labor in which he toils under the
> sun during the few years of his life which God has given him;
> for this is his reward. . . . [F]or every man to whom God has
> given riches and wealth, He has also empowered him to eat

from them and to receive his reward and rejoice in his labor; this is the gift of God. (Ecclesiastes 5:18-19)

But this principle is not a universal experience in Scripture or in history. By God's design, life can be hard.

Third, God sometimes puts us in a position of standing alone, even against the advice of godly counselors. I believe that when he does that, he increases the volume of his voice so that the person who has to endure that position can stand firm in confidence.[12] Though Jeremiah had temporary allies, there were very few truly sympathetic people around him, Baruch perhaps being his only close companion. There's no reason to believe that everyone who speaks in the Lord's name today will be well received if they're true servants of God.

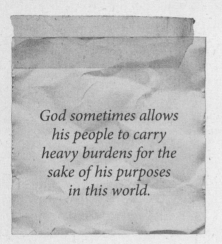

*God sometimes allows his people to carry heavy burdens for the sake of his purposes in this world.*

Jeremiah reveals God's heart in ways that most evangelical Christians would not be able or desire to do. Though we tell each other that God has a wonderful plan for our lives and he wants us to live our best lives now, sometimes God has radically different definitions of what a "wonderful" and "best" life is. Sometimes his heart is grieved and torn over the sins and traumas of his people, and the only way for him to express that grieving heart to the world is through people who will feel it on his behalf. And when feeling God's emotions gets intertwined with the personal life and experiences of his prophetic people, these servants experience a lot of distress and isolation. We see this in people whose hearts ache over the issue of abortion, who serve sacrificially by pouring their lives out in drug- and gang-infested communities, and so on. We can lessen the distress by embracing those with the unusual calling of expressing the excruciating sentiments of God, just as we warmly receive those who portray his joy. And if God leads us in ways that alarm us or wrench our desires from us against our will, we can trust that we aren't missing out on some idealized Christian life everyone else seems to be experiencing. Deep inside the redeemed soul are pains that fit God's purposes because they have the awesome privilege of expressing his own heart.

## FORGOTTEN MESSAGES FROM JEREMIAH:

+ Sometimes God has us swimming against the stream our whole lives—and feeling like we're going to drown at any moment.
+ Often God's promises for an abundant life are realized both in this age and the next, but not always. Sometimes it's just the next. God's perspective on our abundant life looks at all of eternity simultaneously.[13]
+ Deeply distressed people may be crazy. Or they may be divinely inspired. Or maybe even a little of both. Jeremiah is a case study in why we shouldn't try too hard to sort that out.

# CHAPTER 17

# A FEW LOOSE WHEELS

Online transcript from tonight's news:

**MELISSA SHADRICK (REPORTER):** In tonight's KBBN-TV in-depth feature, we turn our attention to Zadok ben-Adam ben Buzi. Investigated this week under suspicion of homicide, the enigmatic Zadok has still not been charged with a crime . . . not even a misdemeanor. But many are beginning to wonder, *Who is this man?*

Our story begins with the influx of refugees into our city after the first Gulf War. Among those refugees? The mysterious Zadok. With unflinching convictions and nerves of steel, he began making controversial statements almost immediately—not about his new home, but about his homeland and his people. Soon his comments developed a dramatic flair—and that's when the refugees he loved turned their backs on him. One former friend describes the change.

**FORMER FRIEND (ENGLISH TRANSLATOR'S VOICE-OVER):** We used to love him, of course. Everyone did because he stood up for us. But something happened. One day he was our friend. The next day he was God's. And he would never again try to be both.

**MELISSA:** What happened? Do you know?

**FORMER FRIEND:** No. He tried to tell us, but we could not understand him. He saw something . . . something very strange. Something that changed the look in his eyes forever.

**MELISSA:** Those who knew him then say Zadok quit speaking altogether unless, as he describes it, "the voice of God came through." And that voice, apparently, was often insulting and divisive. But even when "the voice" was silent, the self-proclaimed prophet got his message across. Officer Phil Murdock explains . . .

**MURDOCK:** He had an uncanny knack for disturbing the peace without actually doing anything illegal . . . so it was real hard to charge him with anything. He'd stop about an inch short of breaking the law. And as much as I wish you could arrest somebody for weirdness, you can't.

**MELISSA:** That "weirdness" has defied the expectations of many in this city for years. Every day for well over a year, Zadok lay on the sidewalk in the public square as faithfully as a nonunion worker with no sick leave. Why? To make a point to his countrymen: they were refugees because they had abandoned God—one year for every day he lay still on the concrete. On another occasion, he built a campfire on the sidewalk using manure—the one time he received a citation for violating a city ordinance—and proceeded to grill his lunch over the fire. These and many other antics used to be the butt of jokes. But in light of the death of Zadok's wife last week, they now raise serious questions. Law enforcement has come under considerable scrutiny for ignoring the red flags that seem to pop up wherever Zadok goes. But as the chief of police insisted at his news conference yesterday, there's nothing more that officials can do when no crime has been committed. I asked the chief afterward about the force's inability to stop the man with "the voice."

**POLICE CHIEF:** Sure, it's frustrating. We know he had something to do with it. I mean, he very publicly said one morning that his wife was going to die, and then that afternoon, she was dead. That would almost qualify as a confession if the sequence of events didn't matter.

**MELISSA:** Is there any other evidence?

**POLICE CHIEF:** No, that's the problem. He has a history of mental illness and a dead spouse, so obviously we have a suspect. But other than that prediction, we have no evidence. No drugs in her body, no sign of foul play, no evidence of a struggle, nothing. He wasn't even there when it happened. That's just not enough for the courts.

**MELISSA:** You mentioned mental illness. I'm sure many are wondering, Why didn't the state try to have him committed to an institution at some point over the years?

**POLICE CHIEF:** It's very difficult to have someone committed against his will these days, much harder than it used to be. You have to be able to demonstrate that the person in question is a potential danger to himself or others. We never had any evidence for that . . . well, until now, I guess.

**MELISSA:** So the enigma remains while the investigation continues. Zadok has not gone into hiding, as many expected. Just the opposite, in fact; he continues his dramatic interpretations and those harsh messages from "the voice" wherever he can draw a crowd. Now integrated into society, the former refugees don't gather around to listen as they once did—not even to mock him. Apparently, this is one act that has worn thin—and, in the eyes of many, become very disturbing. That's all from the square. Donna, back to you.

**DONNA, NEWS ANCHOR:** Thanks, Melissa. Fascinating report. Now let's take a look at tomorrow's weather forecast . . .

+ + + +

Ezekiel was the poster prophet for neurotic behavior. He wasn't actually neurotic, of course—or if he was, it was by God's design—but he would appear that way to us if we observed him. I've read theories that he was a catatonic schizophrenic, manic-depressive, or a victim of various other severe mental disorders.[1] He was more than just eccentric; he was so unpredictable that some of us would consider him potentially dangerous. We'd certainly keep the kids away.

As the fictional transcript of this news feature indicates, the modern equivalent of Ezekiel would be a foreigner wandering the streets of a refugee community and acting out messages of wrath and hope in order to explain why they had to leave their home country. To us, he'd have the appearance of an inner-city homeless man—at least during those times he was lying on streets or grilling his food over dung. If we encountered him on the streets, we might assume he was profoundly and permanently impacted by the drug culture of the sixties, and we wouldn't be too surprised to see him hoisting a sign proclaiming that "The End Is Near." Understanding the culture of Ezekiel's time might lessen our shock a little, but not much. He was essentially as strange to his people as he would be to us.

For those who aren't familiar with Ezekiel's story, he was one of the early exiles taken to Babylon from Jerusalem more than a decade before its destruction. While Jeremiah prophesied God's impending judgment to the people in Jerusalem, Ezekiel prophesied to the captives already in Babylon. His message was often painful and harsh, but like Jeremiah, he foresaw the end of judgment and the hope of restoration and blessing.

We've already mentioned a couple of examples of his odd behavior and prophetic perceptions, but here's a more complete list:

+ He built a model of the siege of Jerusalem out of clay tablets and iron pans in order to give the exiles a visual picture of their judgment.[2]

+ He lay on his left side for 390 days to bear the burden of 390 years' worth of Israel's sin; then he lay on his right side for 40 days for Judah's sin.

+ During his illustrations of siege and sin-bearing, he bared his arm and prophesied in the direction of Jerusalem while being bound by ropes.

+ He was instructed to make bread from six ingredients[3] and cook it over excrement. This would be his food during his public siege demonstration. Why? To point out to the exiles that they would have to eat defiled (nonkosher) food in a foreign country until their judgment was over.

+ He shaved his head and beard, divided almost all of the hair into three piles, then burned one inside his model city, whacked at the second pile with his sword, and then scattered the third bunch in the wind. He saved a few strands, however, to sew into the hem of his garments.

+ He dug a hole in a wall and crawled through it to illustrate how Jerusalem's leaders would be led away into exile.[4]

+ He told parables in graphic detail, including explicit descriptions of such images as a baby squirming in its afterbirth[5] and a lust-filled prostitute.[6]

+ As an illustration of God's relationship with his people, Ezekiel predicted his wife's death, which, to outside observers, would have looked awfully suspicious.[7]

+ He wrote the names of Israel and Judah on two sticks and joined them together to tell everyone that the divided kingdoms would be reunited one day.

+ He had visions in which he ate a scroll, boiled a pot full of meat and bones as an illustration of burning out impurities, prophesied to the breath of life and watched dry bones turn into people again, and toured two versions of the Temple while commenting in excruciating detail.
+ His visions of God have been admired by psychedelic poets and UFO enthusiasts alike.[8]

In terms of personality, we can identify many of the same characteristics in Ezekiel that we did in Jeremiah. Both seemed, from a purely human perspective, to frequently be depressed, to isolate themselves (or be isolated by others) in degrees that could be considered antisocial, to speak of God's wrath with irritating frequency, to use graphic metaphors, to have an unnatural need to be at the center of attention, and to ignore the advice of others. However, Ezekiel didn't seem to have the same timidity, introspection, and desire to avoid conflict that Jeremiah did. He may not have enjoyed the confrontational aspects of his ministry, but he didn't cringe from them to the degree that his contemporary did. Perhaps more than any other biblical figure, he fits our stereotype of the wild-eyed, judgment-declaring, in-your-face prophet.

There's a young Jewish man who wanders our neighborhood constantly. I know he's Jewish because most people in this neighborhood are and because I've never seen him without his yarmulke. He frequently seems to be talking to himself, and he always seems to be on a mission. He takes brisk walks with no discernible pattern to them, but he always stops in various stores and restaurants, makes a few gestures, and then turns around and leaves as abruptly as he entered. His countenance looks normal, but

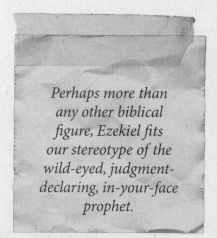

*Perhaps more than any other biblical figure, Ezekiel fits our stereotype of the wild-eyed, judgment-declaring, in-your-face prophet.*

his behavior isn't; he acts like someone who's mentally ill. But the fact that I can't tell for sure always makes me think of Ezekiel—a devout Jew with extremely odd habits that make you think, *Hmmm, I wonder what that guy's problem is.* That, in a nutshell, had to be the response of many people when they saw the son of Buzi doing his thing in Babylon.

I can't imagine anyone in evangelicalism today having an open mind toward Ezekiel. And though I admire him tremendously as a biblical prophet and consider his book one of my favorites in the Bible, I would be one of the first to be offended by his words, his actions, or even the fact that he was sitting in a pew next to me. In real life, it would not even enter my mind that perhaps this guy could be a spokesman for God—that the Father I'm so familiar with would be operating in and through such an offbeat personality. That in itself is somewhat disturbing to me; knowing that I would want to distance myself from someone God had gotten pretty close to is more than a little alarming. The Father and I would not be on the same page.

> *Knowing that I would want to distance myself from someone God had gotten pretty close to is more than a little alarming.*

Not only is it hard to imagine having an open mind toward Ezekiel, it's hard to imagine how we would advise him. I wouldn't know where to start. If he were a member of a Christian family, there would be serious discussions about institutionalizing him. If he were a member of a church, there would be concerted efforts to keep him off committees and away from the kids. Most pastors would understandably treat him as a thorn in their side, and most congregation members would disassociate with him during fellowships and worship services. If any contingent from the church tried to help him live a normal lifestyle and develop decent relationships, he would rebuff them rather quickly and tell them not to obstruct God's message. Ezekiel would be tolerated—barely—only because the church has an obligation to tolerate everyone.

If you think I'm exaggerating the case against Ezekiel, try reading chapters 4 and 5 while imagining someone you know in the role of the prophet. Ask yourself, *How would I react to someone doing these things in public? What would I say to someone who claimed to speak for God as often as Ezekiel did?*[9] *How would I feel about being a family member or friend of someone who was a celebrity simply for the lurid things he said and the embarrassing acts he performed? Could I handle having my reputation affected by my association with the butt of talk-show jokes and/or my occasional appearance in the tabloid photos of his rabid behavior?* If you're truly able to picture the situation and allow yourself to feel discomfort from the spotlight on Ezekiel's life, you'll understand: this great man of God was not great at all in the eyes of most of his contemporaries.

The point, of course, is that God often shows up in disguise, and sometimes that disguise is the last thing we would expect. I believe God sometimes even packages his truth in offensive or irritating ways to see if we're hungry enough to accept it anyway. There's no better way to hone a gift of discernment than to practice separating issues of truth from issues of packaging. Sometimes truth and its medium are obviously linked, but sometimes they aren't. That's why Samuel wasn't able to recognize David as the future king of Israel simply by looking at his outward appearance[10] and why many people never recognized Jesus as the Messiah. The packaging wasn't what they expected, and they couldn't separate the medium from the message. Stereotypes can lead to tragic rejections in the Kingdom of God.

Most Christians encountering an Ezekiel today would tell him to get help. Elijah and John the Baptist would fit in this category too—people whose issues are so far outside of our own experience that we'd be at a loss as to how to approach them. If we wanted to deal with them ourselves, we'd probably tell them that God would not inspire such crazy behavior, that being a recluse is outside the will of God—there are no lone rangers in the Kingdom of God because we're designed for fellowship, right?—

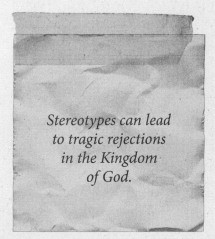

*Stereotypes can lead to tragic rejections in the Kingdom of God.*

and that they sure don't look like they believe that "God is love." And all of our advice would be based on Scripture. But few of us would even try to say these things, convinced that what they really need is professional help.

Once again, we face this issue of the difference between having *the* biblical principles versus having *some* biblical principles. Counseling someone against crazy behavior, lone-ranger faith, and harsh representations of God is certainly biblical advice. In most cases, it's absolutely the right word for the right occasion. But it isn't always. Sometimes it's the wrong biblical advice, and we have to come to grips with the fact that there is such a thing—that "wrong biblical" advice is not an oxymoron. Solidly biblical principles can be rightly applied in one situation and wrongly applied in another, and the variables between those situations are sometimes invisible to human discernment.

Peter is a good example of this difficulty. He found himself in the awkward position of explaining to the Messiah that the Messiah was supposed to conquer, not be conquered. Jesus had foretold his crucifixion, and Peter had heard quite a few prophecies of the Messiah's ultimate victory. And those prophecies were right; Peter had a correct biblical understanding of the Messiah's ultimate role. But in his protests over Jesus' pessimism, he was misapplying biblical truth. And Jesus' response was not gentle: "Get behind Me, Satan!" (Matthew 16:21-23). That's God's assessment of our blanket applications of what we think is *the* biblical perspective—in this case, the clear biblical truth that the Messiah would conquer and rule. There was another biblical perspective that fit this situation, but only the Spirit could have opened Peter's eyes to it. Jesus considered the source of Peter's Scripture-based advice to be satanic.

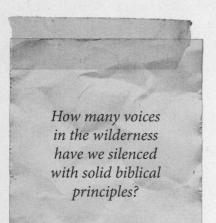

*How many voices in the wilderness have we silenced with solid biblical principles?*

How many times do you think we as a church have given people scriptural advice that would hinder God's calling in their lives? How many voices in the wilderness have we silenced with solid biblical principles? I'm pretty sure I've counseled people to be obedient to a truth in God's Word when God's voice was leading them in a direction contrary to my understanding of Scripture.[11] That's what happens when our relationship with God becomes merely a religion—when we put our faith on automatic pilot and stop listening for the subtleties of his voice. We must be absolutely unmovable with regard to the static truths of the Bible: the nature of God in all three persons, the way of salvation, and the inspiration of Scripture, for example. But regarding the directives of commandments and prophecies that must be applied in specific situations, we need to discern the dynamics. How do we define appropriate behavior for a servant of God? How do we define *sanity* in someone who's being guided by an invisible and unpredictable Spirit? When we anchor ourselves to our own understanding of God's unchanging Word, assuming we know how it applies to each and every circumstance, we can miss the moment he has planned for us. We're blinded to the time of our visitation.

Our role as servants and children of God is to listen to the Father's voice, which most often comes to us through Scripture. But it comes not as a code of conduct or a set of precepts but as a dynamic voice that says, "This is my will in this particular situation. Draw close to me and pay attention." This requires two-way communication, which God offers to anyone with the wisdom to ask for it and the patience to learn how to hear him. He answers prayers that ask for "the eyes of your heart" (Ephesians 1:18) to be opened further. It is possible to hear him clearly and confidently.[12] And this dynamic fellowship with God will save us from the errors of assumption, but only when we carefully cultivate that fellowship. Intimate communion with God is the key to hearing his voice.

## FORGOTTEN MESSAGES FROM EZEKIEL:

+ God often shows up in disguise. Sometimes the disguise is offensive. Therefore, it's never legitimate to rule out the possibility that God spoke simply because the delivery was unappealing, bizarre, or ostensibly the product of mental illness.
+ God often speaks in very visual ways.
+ God's Spirit can fill us with anger.[13]
+ Prophecies of gloom and doom do not contradict God's love.
+ We have a better chance of hearing God's voice if we are interacting with him moment by moment.

# CONCLUSION

Most Christian books don't end this way. Few sermons, Sunday school classes, small-group studies, discipleship groups, and media programs draw the conclusion that whatever sounds deceptive, seems sinful, smells fishy, and looks weird just might be from God. Rare is the counselor or adviser who will tell you that in order to really be used by God, you have to become weak and foolish. It is, admittedly, a very unlikely message. But, then, so is the Bible.

The truth is that though the book ends here, the examples don't. What should we say of a man who spends decades building a massive ship with no shore in sight?[1] Of a woman who tricks her father-in-law to sleep with her in order to establish her legacy among the people of God—and ends up in the Messiah's genealogy?[2] Of a general who leads his ragtag army around a walled city for a week and expects the walls to fall?[3] Of another general who pares his army down to three hundred soldiers so he can get in just the right position to defeat an enemy tens of thousands strong?[4] Of a prophet who challenges pagan priests to a spiritual duel on top of a mountain—just him against 850, to the death?[5] Of a godly apostle who calls an antagonist a child of the devil,[6] casts a demon out of a girl who happens to be annoying him,[7] and walks right back into a city from which he had been dragged out, stoned, and left for dead?[8] Of a Savior who goes to his execution willingly?

These are heroes of faith who lived all-out, regardless of the opinions of others and the potential harm to their own lives. They were unwise and reckless by the world's standards, but

> By faith [they] conquered kingdoms, performed acts of righteousness, obtained promises, shut the mouths of lions, quenched the power of fire, escaped the edge of the sword, from weakness were made strong, became mighty in war, put foreign armies to flight. Women received back their dead by resurrection; and others were tortured, not accepting their release, so that they might obtain a better resurrection; and

others experienced mockings and scourgings, yes, also chains and imprisonment. They were stoned, they were sawn in two, they were tempted, they were put to death with the sword; they went about in sheepskins, in goatskins, being destitute, afflicted, ill-treated (men of whom the world was not worthy), wandering in deserts and mountains and caves and holes in the ground. (Hebrews 11:33-38)

We look back at these faith heroes and laud them for their risk-taking, their focus in listening to God rather than the vast majority of people around them, and their stubborn persistence to believe a promise. We preach sermons about how they stood up to evil and gave up their lives. We hold them up as examples of going against the flow and being bold enough to be different. Yet when we encounter those same characteristics in people we know, we try to reform them.

Why? We have a lot of false expectations—biblically derived expectations about what it means to be godly, which usually translate into "conventional" and "respectable." We take scriptural truth, baptize it in the waters of our culture, and present it to each other and to the world as mature discipleship. And for the most part, it's good. But it isn't always right.

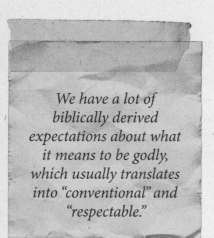

*We have a lot of biblically derived expectations about what it means to be godly, which usually translates into "conventional" and "respectable."*

I know the objections these ideas attract. One is that I've taken isolated incidents from the lives of biblical characters and tried to make a theology out of them. As one colleague once told me, "Stop pulling out the most unusual events and stick to the overall message of Scripture!" But I think the overall message of Scripture is that such unusual events are commonplace to God. Whether these specific examples are repeatable or not is beside the point. I would agree with anyone who tells me there won't be another mountaintop sacrifice of an only son or a symbolic marriage to a prostitute or a virgin birth. The point is that no one can say, "God wouldn't do something like that. That just isn't like him." The fact is that he did these things, and it *is* like him to do them. These were his ideas that flowed out of his heart because they were consistent with his character. It's doubtful that he'll speak through another burning bush or tell anyone else to build an ark, but it's possible—even likely—that these *kinds* of things will come up again in the lives of people whose minds are open to the possibilities. He can work powerfully through one person who lives an ordinary, conventional-looking life and then direct another person to live contrary to those ordinary conventions. It's his choice. Though he often appears very tame, he isn't.

> *God can work powerfully through one person who lives an ordinary, conventional-looking life and then direct another person to live contrary to those ordinary conventions.*

Neither can anyone relegate these people and events to the past and say God isn't like that anymore. God doesn't change. If he was comfortable with things that were bizarre to us in the past, he's comfortable with them now. He's under no obligation to fit our cultural expectations. The real question here is whether Scripture shows us examples to follow or exceptions to admire but never to expect. I think the latter makes no sense. Why would God give us a Bible full of wild, astounding miracles and marvels and then say, "But I don't do this anymore. Sorry." That's not compassionate, it's cruel. No, Scripture emphatically declares that the new covenant is better than the old.[9] To say that God no longer works as he did in the Bible is to say the opposite.

One might argue further that my descriptions of biblical situations in this book haven't been very realistic, as I acknowledged up front. Obviously, something will always be lost in translation when you take people and events from thousands of years ago and place them in today's world. But I would counter that the tension in the lives of these people is represented accurately in the scenarios in which I've placed them. The dynamics of their circumstances weren't over as quickly as it takes to read the few verses that tell about them now. They were excruciating, intense, confusing, and often frightening in real time. We happen to know that God was with them—the ends of their stories vindicate the beginnings—so there's no suspense as we read them. But God's vindication was not at all clear at the time. Most of these characters wrestled with fears, many of them wondering if God had really spoken to them, most of them in the unfortunate position of being either rejected or ridiculed by the people around them. In each of their cases, society didn't recognize God at work. His role was inside information to those who experienced it and who would suffer at society's hands for it—even when "society" was made up of people who followed God and considered themselves spiritually mature.

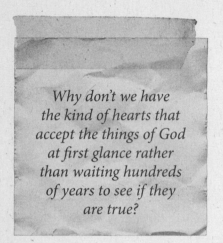

*Why don't we have the kind of hearts that accept the things of God at first glance rather than waiting hundreds of years to see if they are true?*

Why don't we have the kind of hearts that accept the things of God at first glance rather than waiting hundreds of years to see if they are true? Why aren't we open to his movements on the spot? It isn't because God won't show himself. He promises to reveal himself to any who are sincere in their desire to know and discern and understand him. No, we close our hearts to him when we think we understand him already. Once we've learned a certain truth, we don't want any future voices confusing the matter—even when that voice is God's. Most Christians today—and, in fact, throughout history—have desperately wanted the Lion of Judah to be tame.

He isn't, of course.[10] When we first become aware of that, it's a little unsettling. Over time, however, it actually becomes comforting. We don't have to figure out his patterns and bear the burden of making our lives fit perfectly into his plan. We need to fit his character, of course—to be conformed to the image of Christ, to be more precise. We can rest in the fact of who he is and know that eternal truth doesn't change. But the application of eternal truth in real life is trickier, and no matter how much we try to calculate our place in his Kingdom, he's going to surprise us fairly often. And think about it: isn't that the way we'd rather live? Life with the Spirit of God is an adventure, a vast landscape before us with unpredictable turns in every path. There's a very narrow gate to enter, but the pastures in his Kingdom are immense and varied. And we don't have to figure out how to navigate them; it's enough to ask him to take us wherever he wants us to go. Then we trust him to do that and hang on. He'll stretch us, bend us, startle us, blow our minds, and bring us into places we never could have designed for ourselves. It's a thrilling ride.

That's why it's vitally important to question our myths today. The Spirit of God is moving, and his activity is visibly increasing. In the coming days and years, he will break us out of our expectations. That has always been his

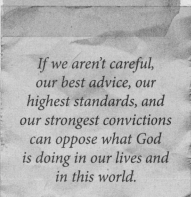

*If we aren't careful, our best advice, our highest standards, and our strongest convictions can oppose what God is doing in our lives and in this world.*

pattern in Scripture and in church history, and it's certain to continue. If we cling stubbornly to evangelical culture and traditions as we know them, treating them as sacred rather than as simply helpful, we'll miss him. Our best advice, our highest standards, and our strongest convictions can, if we aren't careful, oppose what he is doing in our lives and in this world. We have to expect the unexpected and allow ourselves to be stretched. God is fitting us for a Kingdom that is beyond anything we can ask or imagine. Only hearts that are willing to expand, even uncomfortably, will be able to enjoy it now.

# NOTES

## INTRODUCTION

1. See also Marvin R. Wilson, *Our Father Abraham* (Grand Rapids: Wm. B. Eerdmans Publishing Co., 1989), 205.

2. I cling to those doctrines that involve (1) the nature of God (including the Trinity and the deity of Jesus); (2) the means of salvation (justification by grace through faith in Christ); and (3) the inspiration and authority of Scripture, which, though prone to a variety of interpretations, is God's revelation of eternal truth. These core beliefs are, in my opinion, a bare minimum for defining orthodox Christianity, as I'll emphasize later as well.

3. 2 Peter 2:10, 18

4. 1 John 2:17

5. Psalm 37:4

6. John 15:7 (also John 14:13-14; 15:16; 16:23-26)

7. I'm not proposing situational ethics, at least not in the sense of applying true biblical absolutes selectively. The situational nature of our principles applies to those we only think are biblical.

8. From a *Time* magazine review of *Wishful Thinking: A Theological ABC*, http://www.time.com/time/magazine/article/0,9171,907053,00.html.

9. John 3:8. I realize that in this verse Jesus is speaking specifically about how the Spirit brings people to saving faith; however, I believe this is the particular application of a larger truth—that this is how the Holy Spirit works in general.

10. I'm intentionally not using the term *systematic theology* very precisely here—at least not in a formal, academic sense—because we all have a systematic theology to some degree. Formally, systematic theology draws truths and principles and doctrines out of the narratives and discourses of the Bible, which did not come to us in very systematic form at all. Theologians do this on a grand scale, but we all do it some, and in most cases, we do it rather appropriately. For example, we read of the Red Sea parting, we draw some conclusions about God's character (like "He's a merciful deliverer"), and we add that to our descriptive profile of who God is. That's good and right, but when this profile becomes the extent of our understanding of God, we have head knowledge about God's character without having any "Red Sea" experiences ourselves. And that's where God prefers to interact with us—in experience and at a heart level.

11. 2 Corinthians 3:6

12. I realize that I've assumed the role of a troubleshooter in this book, so there's some level of hypocrisy in my complaint. I do admit a need for watchdogs of the faith; I just want to make sure they're watching the right things, barking only at the dangers worth barking about, and not trying to chase the Holy Spirit off of their turf.

13. Though no teacher in Jesus' day would have considered himself to think like a Greek, Judaism had been dramatically affected by Greek culture over the previous three centuries. This was certainly true of "Hellenized Jews"—those scattered across the Roman empire—but even the religious leaders in Jerusalem who were still distinctively Hebrew weren't quite as distinctive as they thought. The Hellenization of Jewish thought and logic had long been underway.

14. See also Genesis 9:4; Leviticus 3:17; 6:30; 7:26-27; 17:10-14; 19:26; Deuteronomy 12:16, 23-25; 15:23; 1 Samuel 14:32-34; Ezekiel 33:25.

15. Though I imply that these tensions contradict our biblical understanding, they don't actually contradict the Bible. In fact, there's plenty of biblical evidence that God uses foolish, unexpected, logic-defying vehicles for his works.

16. Matthew 11:2-4

17. A biblical example of this is the Judaizers whom Paul battled so fiercely. They were professing Christians who clung to the Old Testament expectation that anyone who comes to God, including Gentiles, should observe the laws of the Torah. They are a historical footnote today because unlike Peter and James in Acts, who didn't understand how or why the Spirit was falling upon Greeks but saw clearly that he was, they didn't grasp the Spirit's surprising work in the Gentile world.

## CHAPTER 1: CREATIVE INTERPRETATION

1. In John 12:32, Jesus says, "And I, if I am lifted up from the earth, will draw all men to Myself." This picture of lifting Jesus up has been used in discussions of praising and exalting the Savior as it relates to evangelistic witness and mission efforts. In the next verse, John specifies the intent of Jesus' statement: "He was saying this to indicate the kind of death by which He was to die." As we'll see, the primary meaning of this passage relates to Jesus' death on the Cross—but it's not the only possible application.

2. Isaiah 6:9-10

3. Matthew 13:14

4. Hosea 11:1

5. Matthew 2:15

6. Compare Micah 7:6 with Matthew 10:35-36

7. Compare Jeremiah 31:15 with Matthew 2:18

8. Zechariah 11:12, quoted in Matthew 27:9 but prefaced by "that which was spoken through Jeremiah the prophet." This is explainable by the fact that the book at the beginning of a scroll was often used as the title for the whole scroll, even though several books were in the collection. A "Jeremiah" scroll could easily contain the works of several minor prophets as well and be referred to as "that which was spoken by Jeremiah (the book)" as opposed to Jeremiah (the prophet). Still, this looks careless on Matthew's part and would not comply with our hermeneutical standards today.

9. I wish I could remember the verse he said she cited so I could see how she derived the specific time element, but I wasn't able to write it down and have now forgotten it.

10. These methods of interpretation were perhaps formalized in the classical rabbinic period (after AD 70), but their foundations are much earlier than that. These methods of interpretation—all four, but *sod* to a lesser extent—are evident in the apocryphal books of the intertestamental period; the Oral Torah (Mishnah); writings attributed to Philo, an Alexandrian Jew; the pre-Christian literature discovered at Qumran; and even the later Old Testament's use of earlier Old Testament books. On the latter, Benjamin Sommer writes, "Priests and prophets, psalmists and scribes composed Scripture by recycling Scripture, by turning it and turning it to find new truths in it. For many biblical writers, new words from God emerged from intense examination and reordering of the old ones. The interpretation of a sacred text could yield revelation, as much as revelation yielded a sacred text. If this is so, then the gulf that separates the Bible or *Torah shebikhtav* ("Written Torah") from rabbinic tradition or *Torah sheb'al peh* ("Oral Torah") is smaller than one might think" (from "Early Nonrabbinic Interpretation" in Adele Berlin, Mark Zvi Brettler, Michael Fishbane, eds., *The Jewish Study Bible* [New York: Oxford University Press, 2004], 1838). Sommer further writes that "Midrash, then, is not just a postbiblical invention used by the Rabbis to revise the Bible as they saw fit. It is a biblical means of relating to the Bible, which the Rabbis inherited from the biblical authors themselves" (p. 1832) and that the Rabbis followed scriptural precedent in "purposefully misquoting" scriptural passages (p. 1833).

11. The writer of Hebrews, for example, goes well beyond allegory (*midrash*)—and beyond a brief reference in Psalm 110:4—in comparing Jesus with Melchizedek in Hebrews 7. His treatment of Genesis 14 requires a *sod* approach to describe the hidden connection between them. Paul's allegory of Hagar and Sarah as representative of two covenants, a *midrash*, also has elements of *sod* in it. And John employs this approach, plus ample *remezim*, quite frequently in Revelation as he draws out hidden meaning (and adds some more) in multiple implicit and subtle references to Ezekiel, Isaiah, and other Old Testament texts.

12. You'll notice in some of the sample verses from Matthew above that the Gospel writer is simply quoting Jesus' application of an Old Testament verse.

13. Isaiah 64:4

14. Most notable among biblical examples of God-ordained chaos is the day of Pentecost, which hardly any human being would describe as "orderly." It is described in Acts 2 in words that indicate mass confusion—various languages being spoken simultaneously as a multiethnic crowd clamors in bewilderment and amazement. Only when Peter stands up and begins to clarify the situation does the disorder subside. From God's perspective, this confusion went exactly according to plan.

## CHAPTER 2: THE MOSTLY TRUE PROPHET

1. By "prophet," I mean anyone who is able to hear the Lord's voice and deliver his message to a particular people in a particular situation. This, of course, includes the Old Testament prophets—those who wrote, like Isaiah, as well as those who didn't, like Elijah and Elisha—but also those who perform that function

regardless of whether they ever hold that title. There are companies or schools of prophets in the Old Testament history books and a widespread prophetic practice in Acts and the New Testament church. In fact, in 1 Corinthians 14:1 (NIV), Paul urges everyone to "eagerly desire"—or, more literally, to "earnestly covet"—the gift of prophecy, as though it's available to and expected of all Christians.

2. For example, the new heavens and new earth are understood by most theologians to be a picture of life after Jesus' return—a life unaffected by death (Revelation 21:1-4). Yet in Isaiah 65:20, the new heavens and new earth are filled with people who die at a ripe old age. We don't doubt the truth of what Isaiah sees; but we would love some sort of explanation as to how it all fits together.

3. Isaiah, along with many other prophets, fills his writing with phrases like, "This is what the LORD says." Regardless of how arrogant it may sound to suggest that your words are actually God's words, Peter insists that this is the case: "If anyone speaks, he should do it as one speaking the very words of God" (1 Peter 4:11, NIV).

4. Isaiah 60–66 in particular are filled with visions of the far-off realization of the ultimate Kingdom of God. But even his more "immediate" prophecies of the suffering servant Messiah would not be fulfilled for several more centuries.

5. Isaiah 20. Though his degree of clothing can certainly be interpreted as something less than completely naked, the prophet is still embarrassingly bare.

6. Isaiah 8:1-3

7. 2 Chronicles 32:24-26; 2 Kings 20:1-7; Isaiah 38:1-8. Isaiah actually prophesied twice regarding Hezekiah's illness, first declaring emphatically that the king would not recover, then, at the Lord's instructions following Hezekiah's repentance, reversing the decision. This seems perfectly acceptable to us in retrospect, but imagine a preacher predicting the future today and then backtracking a few days (or even a few minutes) later. Would we give him the same latitude?

8. Isaiah 6

9. Compare, for example, the doom and gloom of Isaiah chapters 22 and 24 with the joy of 25–27, or the woes of 29–34 (minus brief highs in 30:18-33 and 32:1-8, 15-20) with the blessings of 35. These prophecies make sense within a certain time line, of course, but, with the time line remaining unexplained, they do leave the reader with a feeling of whiplash.

10. Imagine, for example, the backlash against a preacher today if he publicly predicted widespread suffering in the United States and the eventual overthrow of the country by Iran or Al-Qaeda—not because those entities are supported by God, but because America has sinned. Current balance of power notwithstanding, that's about the flavor of the prophecies of Isaiah and Jeremiah.

11. This is evident in nearly every new Spirit-inspired movement or denomination. Leaders of an established order generally don't respond well to branch-off movements, which results in the kind of criticism and interference people like Peter and John, Francis of Assisi, Martin Luther, William Carey, John and

Charles Wesley, and many more had to endure. The early days of God-initiated transitions are normally pretty contentious.

12. See also in Matthew 13:57 (NIV) the response Jesus got in Nazareth, prompting him to quote a common saying: "Only in his hometown and in his own house is a prophet without honor." We might add, "and only in his time."

13. Jonah 3:4

14. The "prophetic movement," as it is often called, is a burgeoning emphasis on the ministry of God speaking to Christians through other Christians for the purposes described in 1 Corinthians 14:3—to edify, exhort, and encourage. This ministry has always been in the church in varying degrees, but it has been marginalized since the Enlightenment. It's experiencing a revival of sorts, in which Christians believe they can actually speak the very words of God to one another in a timely, supernaturally insightful manner (1 Peter 4:11)—not infallibly, of course, since we all see dimly and partially (1 Corinthians 13:12), but still very effectively.

15. Though timely preaching and writing, especially with regard to justice and other social issues, have always been considered to have prophetic implications, I'm referring specifically to declarations and predictions received by supernatural revelation.

16. One of the most explicit examples of a nonapostle prophesying in the New Testament is Agabus, who on two occasions foretold coming events accurately. In Acts 11:27-28, he predicted a famine that, as it turns out, later took place in the reign of Claudius; and in Acts 21:10-14, he told Paul of the suffering he would undergo in Jerusalem. In the first case, the church acted on the prophecy by taking up an offering for famine relief. In the second, Luke and many fellow believers pleaded with Paul not to go, and though he agreed that the prophecy sounded accurate, he went on to Jerusalem knowing that his ministry there would involve great sacrifice. Interestingly, this same passage is prefaced with a statement about Philip the evangelist having four daughters who were prophetesses (21:9). Paul himself referred to the prophetic gift at least twenty-five times in his letters (in addition to his references to Old Testament prophets), and the context almost always implied a general ability of God's people to hear from the Holy Spirit and speak his words.

17. 1 Thessalonians 5:20

18. John 8:15; 1 Corinthians 2:14-15

## CHAPTER 3: SECONDHAND STORIES

1. Jesus did warn his followers that many deceivers would come in his name doing signs and wonders (Matthew 24:24). This warning, however, is meant to caution us that not everything supernatural is from God; it's about the source of the event, not the event itself. It is not teaching us to explain miracles in naturalistic terms until proven otherwise. Whenever people encountered a miracle in the Gospels, they faced a choice. Those who believed and rejoiced were commended; those who questioned whether a miracle really happened were rebuked.

2. Acts 17:32, for example.

3. Acts 23:6

4. 1 Corinthians 1:25

5. Hebrews 11:6

6. Matthew 17:20

7. Matthew 9:29

8. Matthew 13:57-58

9. C. S. Lewis, *The Lion, the Witch and the Wardrobe* (New York: HarperTrophy, 1950), 51–52.

10. Much of the New Testament was written for the purpose of refuting false teaching. For some specific examples, see 1 Corinthians 2; 2 Corinthians 11; 2 Peter 2; 1 John 4:1-6; and Jude.

11. I realize there's a certain subjectivity with each of these, but spiritual experience always involves subjectivity. It's impossible to truly experience a relationship with God with empirical precision. (Same goes with any human relationship— like marriage, for example. To a degree, you have to assume the truth of the other person's feelings and perceptions.)

## CHAPTER 4: FALLEN BUT NOT FORGOTTEN

1. Since polygamy is illegal, we can't make any realistic comparisons here; but the sexual recklessness of Solomon's life would be staggering even in today's society.

2. The name "Solomon" comes from the word *shalom,* which literally means peace, but includes abundance, fullness, wholeness, completeness, and satisfaction. His kingdom was reflected in his name.

3. The book of Ecclesiastes was written toward the end of Solomon's life.

4. As Paul wrote to the Corinthians, "Be imitators of me, just as I also am of Christ" (1 Corinthians 11:1). Of all people, Christians should understand how a leader's behaviors and attitudes filter down to us; we're actually being made into the exact image of our Leader, who himself is the exact image of God (Hebrews 1:3).

## CHAPTER 5: TREACHEROUS FAITH

1. According to Genesis 25, Abraham did in fact have six more sons through his second wife, Keturah, after Sarah's death. But Isaac was still the son through whom God's promises were fulfilled and the only heir Abraham designated to receive his estate.

2. See Leviticus 20:2-5, for example, as well as Jeremiah's comments that ritual child sacrifice to demonic deities never even entered God's mind (Jeremiah 7:31; 19:5; 32:35). It's clear that Abraham's willingness to sacrifice Isaac and God's sacrifice of Jesus are radically different from ancient civilizations' practices—which Israel eventually took part in—of burning children in the red-hot stone arms of statues of Molech and Baal. The purposes were different, the spiritual principles involved were different, and the results were different. The pagan rituals were tragic, horrifying, and vile. God's sacrificial heart is loving

and redemptive. My point is not to blur the lines between Abraham and pagan rituals, but to point out that our method of determining God's will wouldn't make a distinction. We would probably point to God's condemnation of pagan practices as proof that he couldn't have called Abraham to do what he did. In other words, we would apply these very important verses to a radically different situation because it looked too similar to us. And in so doing, we would have contradicted God's voice.

3. 1 John 4:18

4. An example of this type is Rees Howells, the Welsh missionary known for his powerful intercessory prayers, and his wife. Convinced that God had called them to Africa, they left their infant son irrevocably in the hands of relatives, vowing never to have any parental claim on him again. They reconnected with him in ministry after he graduated from college—and after tens of thousands of African souls had come to the Lord through the parents' work.

5. This was the situation for the "Cambridge Seven"—seven men who abandoned wealth, success, and the fineries of England's culture in 1885 for grueling, obscure evangelistic work in China's interior.

6. I do, however, believe that the heart attitude involved in Abraham's offering is meant to be repeated again and again in our lives.

7. For a better understanding of God's character, you may find *The Knowledge of the Holy* by A. W. Tozer or *Knowing God* by J. I. Packer to be helpful.

## CHAPTER 6: A PROPHETIC HOOKUP

1. English translations of the biblical text leave it uncertain as to whether Gomer was simply an adulteress or an actual prostitute. The prophecy is clear, however, that she was more than unfaithful and immoral and that she was paid for her services (Hosea 2:5; also, the term "play the harlot" occurs nine times in Hosea in the *Revised Standard Version*).

2. This is admittedly a double entendre, as the word *zara* means "sow" or "plant" as well as "inseminate." The suggestive language follows both marriage terminology and agricultural terminology, indicating an intentional intimation.

## CHAPTER 7: PRIDE OR PREJUDICE?

1. In Genesis 37:2, we read that Joseph tended his father's flocks along with his half brothers, Jacob's sons by Bilhah and Zilpah. In rabbinic commentaries, it's assumed that Joseph was assigned to work with the sons of Bilhah and Zilpah because Reuben, the firstborn and therefore "foreman," along with Leah's other sons, didn't like having Daddy's favorite around. Joseph and Benjamin also were left behind when all the brothers were tending sheep in Shechem.

2. Christine Leigh Heyrman, "The First Great Awakening," Divining America, TeacherServe, National Humanities Center (accessed July 20, 2008), http://www.nationalhumanitiescenter.org/tserve/eighteen/ekeyinfo/grawaken.htm.

3. Edith Blumhofer, "The Welsh Revival—1904–1905," *Paraclete* 20, no. 3, summer 1986, accessed July 20, 2008, http://www.joyfulministry.com/welsh.htm.

## CHAPTER 8: THE SCANDAL ON THE FLOOR

1. The spreading of Boaz's "wings" (his garment) over her is a traditional act that's symbolic of God spreading his wings over Israel. In Ruth, it's a fulfillment of Boaz's blessing in Ruth 2:12. But though the act of covering her with his clothes was traditional, the time and place of this encounter was anything but. It's a situation that could be justified by the desire not to put Boaz in a socially awkward position or to embarrass Ruth publicly if he rejected her, but there would have been other ways around these concerns. The story as it's told is intentionally provocative.

## CHAPTER 9: SURE, SHE'S A VIRGIN

1. His brothers, for example, who had lived with him for years before his public ministry, didn't believe in him (John 7:5), though James converted after the Resurrection and became the leader of the Jerusalem church and author of the book of James.
2. A couple of minor details were changed to avoid a more wordy illustration, but the essence of each story actually happened.

## CHAPTER 10: BAD COMPANY

1. Matthew 4:1-11; Hebrews 4:15
2. For example, letting our light shine for others to see our good works has a positive impact (Matthew 5:16); women can affect their husbands without a word (1 Peter 3:1-2); and living beyond reproach in the midst of a perverse generation can cause us to appear as lights for others (Philippians 2:15). Likewise, the queen of Sheba was drawn to Jerusalem and the Temple because of Solomon's wisdom and reputation (1 Kings 10:1-10); Naaman the Syrian was sent to Israel for healing because of the reputation of Elisha (2 Kings 5); and many people were drawn to Jesus because of his goodness. Righteousness is always appealing to hungry hearts and can cause many to want to leave corruption behind them.
3. John 4:7-38
4. Luke 7:37-39
5. The most common response to my point is that Jesus didn't have the same weaknesses we do, so we need more safeguards. I agree with that; we do need more safeguards. But we don't need to cast aspersions on people who, for whatever reason, find it necessary or purposeful to defy our normal safeguards. They haven't broken any commandment or committed any sin by doing as Jesus did. They may or may not be wise in the matter—we don't know because we don't have all the details of their reasoning—but they certainly aren't guilty of sin.
6. Matthew 23:13-33; Luke 11:42-52
7. John 2:13-17
8. 2 Corinthians 12:20; Galatians 5:20
9. Hebrews 5:7
10. Matthew 13:54-57
11. John 14:6, paraphrased
12. John 2:19, paraphrased

13. John 6:49-51, paraphrased
14. John 10:30, paraphrased
15. John 11:26, paraphrased
16. This was also true of Paul, who "boasted" of his authority in Christ (2 Corinthians 10:8), claimed to have unique visions and experiences (2 Corinthians 12:1), and pleaded his own case often. But this is not true boasting; it's a series of truthful statements about the supremacy of God's calling over all other pursuits and about the extravagant claims Jesus himself made about the authority of his followers. Likewise, Christians are often considered "arrogant" for claiming to know the only way to salvation. But to claim less than that would be to compromise the gospel.
17. Proverbs 16:7
18. Jesus pointed out a biblical illustration of this point when he reminded the Pharisees that David was once led to eat consecrated bread—unlawfully—when he was hungry (Matthew 12:3-4). God incarnate endorsed David's illegal act because a higher principle was at work.

## CHAPTER 11: ROGUE EVANGELISM
1. Acts 16:18; 19:11-12
2. Acts 8:1; 9:1-2
3. 1 Thessalonians 1:6-7, for one example.
4. Paul frequently defended his apostleship and his ministry in his letters. See, for example, 1 Corinthians 9:1-7; 2 Corinthians 10:1-2, 8-10; 11:7-11; and 1 Thessalonians 2:1-6.
5. Much of 2 Corinthians (1:8-11; 4:1-18; 6:3-13; 11:23-33; and 12:11-21) seems to be written as an apologetic for the legitimacy of suffering and persecution.
6. Philippians 1:15-18
7. This is most evident in Acts 15:1-2, 22-26 and throughout Galatians, but it also seems to be the background for 1 Corinthians 9:1-18; 2 Corinthians 10:1-18—12:1-18; Philippians 3:1-3; Colossians 2:4-8; 1 Thessalonians 2:1-6; 3:5; 2 Thessalonians 2:1-12; 1 Timothy 1:3-7; 2 Timothy 2:16-18; 3:10-14; and Titus 1:10-16.
8. This objection to moving around is, in fact, the kind of criticism that is still offered by some to itinerant ministers today.
9. Luke records Paul's conversion story three times in Acts (9:1-19; 22:3-16; 26:1-18), and Paul refers to his own transformation frequently in his letters (1 Corinthians 15:9-10; Galatians 1:13-24; Philippians 3:3-12; 1 Timothy 1:15-16).
10. Compare Galatians 2:11-14 with Acts 16:1-3.
11. Philippians 1:15-18
12. Philippians 3:2. I know Paul was talking about false teachers in that passage, but that's essentially what some doctrine hounds amount to. In their efforts to purify the church from theological imprecision, they define theology more narrowly than the Bible does. And that's how biblical theology gets to be unbiblical.
13. Brian McLaren's book *A Generous Orthodoxy* (Zondervan/Youth Specialties, 2004) attempts to accommodate a wide range of theological perspectives but, in my opinion, is a bit *too* generous, resulting in an amorphous orthodoxy that

isn't very clear on some important biblical doctrines. Most of my points in this book aren't directed at doctrine at all; I don't disagree with current conservative, evangelical statements of faith. I'm more concerned with how those doctrines are applied to life—how Bible teaching has been sanitized to portray God differently than he portrays himself in Scripture.

14. There are definitive statements in these portions of Scripture, obviously, but I'm referring to the examples they set rather than the specific instructions they give. We obey commands; we get ideas from examples. There's a difference.

## CHAPTER 12: IMMATURE PRAISE
1. Exodus 34:6-7
2. Ephesians 1:3-14
3. "Above All" by Paul Baloche and Lenny LeBlanc, © 1999 Integrity's Hosanna Music/ASCAP & LenSongs Publishing ASCAP.
4. This is the gist of Philippians 2:5-11; Hebrews 2:9; Revelation 5:12; and numerous other passages that magnify Jesus' exaltation by associating it with his suffering and, either implicitly or explicitly, associate our suffering with our future share in his glory.

## CHAPTER 13: PRINCIPLES OF INEFFECTIVE LEADERSHIP
1. Numbers 16
2. Genesis 12:3
3. Numbers 14:33; 32:13
4. Genesis 15:16

## CHAPTER 14: INFERIOR MOTIVES
1. James 4:3
2. Deuteronomy 10:17

## THAT LOOKS WEIRD
1. 1 Corinthians 1:27-30
2. 2 Corinthians 12:9-10

## CHAPTER 16: HARD LABOR
1. I'm still not vouching for this preacher because I believe his message was unbiblical in several ways. But his character and style were not as unbiblical as we thought they were.
2. We know, of course, that from an eternal perspective, Jeremiah's misery was short-lived. He now enjoys untold blessings in his Father's arms, so the calling wasn't unfair in the long run.
3. For specifics, visit some Web sites like Voice of the Martyrs (http://www.persecution.org) that tell the stories of Christians who have been tortured or killed for their testimony.
4. It's true that his messages come primarily through the Bible, but unless someone

is specifically drawing our attention to verses of correction, we usually overlook them.

5. To read of this prophet's inner torment, see Jeremiah 15:15-18 and 20:7-18. Jeremiah 11:18-23 and 12:6 tell of a plot to kill him by his neighbors, the men of Anathoth—his home town—and of how his own brothers had betrayed him. His friends were waiting for him to slip (20:10). There is hardly a hint in Jeremiah of any faction that supported him. He wasn't even allowed the moral support of a family, having been forbidden to marry and raise children. Literally and figuratively, he "sat alone" (15:17).

6. Proverbs 11:14; 12:15; 15:22. There *is* wisdom in the counsel of many, obviously. But nowhere does God say to go with the majority opinion. We're to listen to counsel and weigh it, not blindly obey it.

7. Jeremiah 20:7

8. Jeremiah 4:10

9. John 15:11; 16:24; 17:13

10. Ecclesiastes 2:24; 3:13; 5:18-19

11. The idea of God warning of disaster is offensive to some because God, in their understanding, wouldn't focus on doom and gloom. This is clearly illogical, though. The disaster itself is the doom and gloom, and we live in a world full of such catastrophic events. They are coming because they have always come. God's warning, in that case, would be a welcome benefit that helps us prepare, not a burden intended to weigh us down.

12. It seems to be a general pattern in Scripture that the bigger and more radical a task, and the greater the opposition expected, the clearer the revelation commanding it becomes—for example, Moses and the burning bush, Isaiah's call, Mary's virginal conception, etc.

13. Jeremiah 29:10-13 seems to indicate this perspective—a passage that was likely much comfort to the prophet who preached it. See also what the Spirit inspired Paul to write in Romans 8:16-21; 1 Corinthians 2:9; and 2 Corinthians 4:16-18.

## CHAPTER 17: A FEW LOOSE WHEELS

1. Researchers in the fields of psychology and psychiatry have long tried to diagnose biblical characters, and Ezekiel is often the easiest target. Prominent among twentieth-century analyses are Edwin Broome, who diagnosed the prophet with paranoid or catatonic schizophrenia; Daniel Merkur—socially functional psychosis; Kelvin Van Nuys—catatonic schizophrenia; Jacob Arlow—temporary schizophrenoid abandonment of reality; Avner Falk—borderline personality disorder; and others. For interesting reading, search the Internet using keywords "Ezekiel" and "psychology" or "psychiatry."

2. This and the next four examples are found in Ezekiel 4–5.

3. These are the six ingredients of "Ezekiel bread" sold in many health-food stores. It's made from wheat, barley, beans, lentils, millet, and spelt, according to Ezekiel 4:9—and, one would hope, *not* cooked according to the specifications of 4:12.

4. Ezekiel 12

5. Ezekiel 16:5-6
6. Ezekiel 23:20-21
7. Ezekiel 24:15-23
8. Again, simple Web searches will provide plenty of interesting reading along these lines. Use keywords "Ezekiel" and "UFO"; and "Ezekiel" and "psychedelic drugs."
9. Ezekiel says "the word of the LORD came to me" fifty-seven times in the course of his writings—and implies the same many more times.
10. 1 Samuel 16:7
11. I'm not suggesting that God's Word and God's voice are opposed to each other, since they obviously have a common identity. Rather, the Bible gives us different angles and different applications of its truth—not contradictory, just multifaceted—and we often assume that the more obvious application is the only one the Bible allows in a situation, when, in fact, it isn't.
12. There are quite a few books in circulation that help Christians learn how to hear God's voice. *Walking with God* by John Eldredge (Thomas Nelson, 2008) is a good one.
13. Ezekiel 3:14

## CONCLUSION

1. Genesis 6
2. Genesis 38
3. Joshua 6
4. Judges 7
5. 1 Kings 18
6. Acts 13:6-12
7. Acts 16:18
8. Acts 14:19-20
9. Hebrews 8:6
10. Obviously, the truth of who God is doesn't change. We need to cling tightly to the essentials of our faith and what God has clearly revealed. But one of the unchanging truths of God, evident from Genesis through Revelation and beyond, is that he defies expectations. The eternally consistent truth about the Holy Spirit is that he blows like an unpredictable wind. So when we say that the Lion of Judah isn't tame, we aren't suggesting that the Father, the Son, or the Spirit has a changing nature. We're saying that it's God's constant nature to work dynamically.

# you've been told not to trust your emotions—

## to rely on what you know rather than what you feel.

Yet you were created in the image of God, which means that many of your feelings are echoes of his own. In *Feeling like God*, Chris Tiegreen traces the character of God throughout Scripture, showing how God reveals himself as a deeply emotional being who longs to connect closely with you. When men and women like Abraham, Hannah, David, and Paul opened their hearts to him, their lives were radically transformed. Discover how your emotions are a bridge drawing you closer to your Savior—and you'll experience the passion of feeling like God does.

"If you're longing to *feel* God's love—not just *know* it—read this book."—**Chip Ingram**, president, teaching pastor, *Living on the Edge*

CP0266

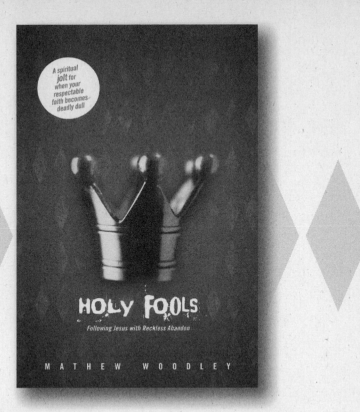

A spiritual **jolt** for when your respectable faith becomes deadly dull

HOLY FOOLS

*Following Jesus with Reckless Abandon*

MATHEW WOODLEY

## *Why settle for complacency when God offers us so much more?*

Mathew Woodley's groundbreaking debut book introduces us to the holy fools (from the desert fathers to Christ himself) who were gutsy enough to push against the grain of society, even to the point of appearing extreme and foolish. Yet God used them to ignite the church to follow Jesus and bring his love to the margins of society—and he can use you in the same way. Ancient and fresh, self-deprecating and honest, *Holy Fools* will shake up your spiritual life and inspire you to pursue a faith without limits.

"A moving and humble book. . . [Woodley's] recasting of Christian dedication as holy folly is appealingly new."—*Library Journal*

"This is the real deal. It challenged me and made me want to grow up."
—Kevin Miller, executive vice president, Christianity Today International

"A literary feast."—Leonard Sweet, professor, Drew Theological School and George Fox University